THE ULTIMATE GOAL SETTING PLANNER

BECOME AN UNSTOPPABLE GOAL ACHIEVER
IN 90 DAYS OR LESS

THIBAUT MEURISSE

INTRODUCTION

Give me a stock clerk with a goal, and I will give you a man who will make history. Give me a man without a goal, and I will give you a stock clerk.

— J.C. PENNY

I'd like to start by thanking you for purchasing this goal-setting planner. It's a big step toward achieving what you want in life, and you're now joining the few people who actually set goals and work on them every day. This alone is cause for celebration.

By committing to using this goal-setting planner on a daily basis, you'll be able to master the skill of goal-setting and gain more control of your life. This will be the best investment you've ever made and, when compounded over the years, the return will be far greater than you could ever imagine.

Setting a 90-Day Goal will allow you to familiarize yourself with the goal-setting process while building momentum toward the achievement of your goals. Whatever your passion, goals, or dreams may be, you'll realize that you can make them a reality.

In this planner, I'll share everything I know about goal-setting in the form of weekly lessons and daily goal-setting tips. This will give you all the tools you need to achieve your goal.

As Jim Rohn used to say. "If you don't design your own life plan, chances are you'll fall into someone else's plan. And guess what they have planned for you? Not much." It's now time for you to design or redesign your own life plan with your passion in mind and more clarity than you've ever had before. I wish you all the best in reaching your goals, and I'm looking forward to interacting with you through this planner.

If you have any questions, feel free to contact me anytime at thibaut.meurisse@gmail.com.

Best wishes,

Thibaut Meurisse

Founder of Whatispersonaldevelopment.org

Before I let you set your own goals we'll discuss the following point:

- What this goal planner is about and why I've created it
- What this planner consists of and how to use it effectively
- Why a 90-Day goal
- How to set exciting goals
- How to work on your goals effectively

To start off on the right foot, make sure you read through all these sections and watched my Welcome video.

WHY THIS GOAL-SETTING PLANNER?

I started setting goals back in 2014 and it has a tremendous impact on my life. This goal-setting planner was created to impact your life in a similar way. Goal-setting enabled me to write the book you're reading right now, among other things. It helped me create my blog and start building my dream career. Nobody told me to start a blog or write books. It was my decision, and I made it happen by setting goals and taking control of my life. While this is easier said than done, I believe that whatever your goal is, there is a way to make it happen.

In fact, the first book I release was on goal-setting, and to my surprise it did well. It helped hundreds and perhaps thousands of people like you to set goals and achieve them. I received great feedback from my readers, which lead me to believe that many people were looking for a way to achieve THEIR goals. Not goals that their parents or society wanted them to achieve, but rather, goals that they were truly passionate about. That's exactly what we'll be working on throughout this planner.

My goal setting book complements the planner and vice versa so for maximum effectiveness feel free to check it out by visiting my Amazon author page at

amazon.com/author/thibautmeurisse.

My Experience with Productivity Planners

In November 2016, I purchased a productivity planner, but I was disappointed by it. I even felt that I could probably make a better one. Progressively I began to realize how much of an impact a good goal-setting planner could actually have on people. If I wanted this sort of product for myself, I reasoned, then maybe others would want it as well.

This is Not Your Average Goal-Setting Planner

When I created this planner, my sole focus was on making a life-changing tool that would significantly impact the lives of those who use it. I wanted you to use this planner to fundamentally reshape your mindset so that you could achieve your goals while adding tremendous value to other people's lives.

Most of what we accomplish in life depends upon our thoughts. An average mindset leads to average results. In the same way, developing an extraordinary mindset will allow you to achieve extraordinary results in your life.

Planner Effectiveness

You might be wondering what makes this planner so effective. There are several things behind this, but the 4 elements below are among the most important.

1. It's structured in a way that allows you to develop a powerful mindset as you progress through your goal-setting journey.

2. It provides you with inspirational quotes and stories that will give you the boost you need to continue working on your goals each and every day.

3. It provides practical daily tips on setting goals. In a matter of months, these tips will make you an expert on setting goals and allow you to double your results in the area you choose to focus on.

4. It includes additional content that will turn you into an unstoppable goal-achiever. This content includes, but is not limited to, the following:

- A comprehensive Daily Morning Ritual guideline and checklist.
- A "Pledge to Become Unstoppable" you can refer to whenever you feel like giving up.
- A list of powerful affirmations sorted by the area they're related to
- A Limiting Beliefs Memo to help you identify your limiting beliefs
- A list of the daily goal-setting tips in the form of a downloadable PDF so you can go over them during your free time.
- A "Beliefs Shifter" section you can use to shift your beliefs
- A "What If" section that will allow you to shift your focus by asking the right questions.
- My Favorite Quotes Section – This is a space to write down your favorite quotes.
- My Thought Bank- A blank section where you can write down any thoughts or ideas that come to you
- Your Quarterly Goal Tracking Sheet to help you keep track of your goals.

This planner also comes with additional bonuses, which you'll find at the following page:

http://whatispersonaldevelopment.org/planner

Read on for a list of the bonuses you can expect.

1. A Tutorial and Welcome Video to help you make the most of this goal-setting planner

2. A weekly video that I've carefully selected to match each section of the planner and give you an extra boost of motivation

3. A series of videos in which I check in on your progress and provide extra advice

4. Several free e-books, all of which are listed below.

- The 5 Commandments of Personal Development
- 7 Proven Strategies to Set Goals You'll Actually Achieve

- Find What You Love: 5 Tips to Uncover Your Passion Quickly and Easily

If for any reason the link doesn't work, make sure to contact me at thibaut.meurisse@gmail.com

The Main Objective

The primary goal of this planner is to help you.

- For starters, it will enable you to identify one exciting goal that you'd like to accomplish within 90 days.
- Secondly, it will provide the insights and inspiration you need to set goals on a daily basis.
- Thirdly, it will help you transform your mindset over time through weekly lessons and daily goal-setting tips.
- Last but not least, it will give you the ability to achieve way more than you previously thought possible.

Your 90-Day Goal

Setting and achieving a 90-Day Goal is one of the primary purposes of this planner. Another purpose is to familiarize you with the process of setting goals. We'll do that by focusing on your most exciting goal right away.. You'll also be provided with the guidance and help needed to develop a mindset that keeps you motivated and sustains your momentum. Once you've mastered the goal-setting process, you can use it to achieve most of the goals you set in the future.

Note that, while your 90-Day Goal may stand on its own, it might also be part of a bigger goal. No matter what your goal is, we'll work on breaking it down into manageable tasks so you can get tangible and measurable results in just 90 days. Sound good? I hope so!

Why Just One Goal?

Most people struggle with maintaining long-term consistency, which poses a major problem when trying to achieve goals. Consistency is particularly challenging in today's world. Distractions are everywhere and there are a multitude of things we could do at any given time. No wonder people can't seem to focus anymore!

Most people have a bad case of "Shiny Object Syndrome", that is, they jump from one diet to another, one get-rich-quick scheme to the next, and generally bounce from thing to thing in multiple areas of their lives.

Sadly, this usually prevents them from achieving much. Once the initial excitement of a new goal wears off, many people are tempted to try the next thing that pops up. Because they can't stick to one thing and commit to mastering it, they're unable to reach even a fraction of their true potential. Yet it's important to overcome this because, as I like to say: The shiny object syndrome is what prevents you from truly shining.

One of the many topics we'll discuss in this book is the notion of mastery, which people like Tony Robbins and Stefan James swear by. Understanding mastery will make a huge difference in your life. It certainly made a difference in mine.

Why 90 Days?

90 days is a long enough time for you to see tangible results as you work toward your goal. It's also enough time for you to familiarize yourself with the goal-setting process and develop a more empowering mindset. It's my sincere hope that you'll continue setting goals after this 90-day period, and ideally for the rest of your life. I'd love to see you make all your goals and dreams come true in the years to come. My vision for you is much bigger than setting and achieving your 90-Day Goal.

Before we work on your 90-Day Goal, however, let's take a look at how this planner works.

HOW TO USE THIS GOAL-SETTING PLANNER

For best results, read through every section of this book. Doing so will help tremendously when it comes to effectively setting short-term and long-term goals.

Is this Planner for Personal or Professional Use?

This planner can be used to achieve personal or professional goals. However, I would encourage you to use it either for personal goals or for professional goals, but not for both. Also, make sure you concentrate [only on one 90-Day Goal.] It's important to see it through before moving to the next one.

Planner Structure

This planner has been designed to provide you with optimum results. To this end, I recommend making the most of each section. You'll be provided with a weekly lesson on a specific topic, such as consistency, procrastination, or failure. Each lesson is based upon my personal experiences and each week will revolve around that specific topic, including relevant quotes and tips to support you as you move towards your goal.

At the beginning of the week, you'll use the weekly planning section to write down the main tasks you need to handle over the next 7 days. Then, you'll set up your daily goals. You'll also review your goal on a monthly basis, which will give you a chance to reflect on the progress you've made and see where you can improve.

Weekly Lessons

I'll provide a new topic every week that will help you develop the mindset needed to achieve your goals. I'll cover topics like beliefs, habits, and self-esteem. These are topics I found critical in my own personal development journey and I think you will, too. I encourage you to follow the lessons in order, but don't hesitate to go back through the previous lessons. Repetition is key when it comes to attaining your goals and achieving success!

Weekly Planning Section

In this section, you'll be given the opportunity to clarify what you want to accomplish during the week by writing down the main tasks you want to complete. Planning is an important element of goal-setting and will save you a lot of time. Brian Tracy goes so far as to say that every minute spent planning saves 10 minutes in executing the plan. By setting your goals for the week, you'll know what to focus and, thus, you'll be able to get things done much faster than you could otherwise.

Daily Goals

Each day you'll be provided with 2 full pages whose structure will be discussed below.

On the 1st page:

Daily Inspirational Quotes

In this section, I've included quotes that are line with the theme of the week. These quotes will help and inspire you on a daily basis.

Main Daily Goals Section:

In this section, you'll write down your daily goals in order of importance. The first goal should be the one most crucial to having a successful day.

When going through this section, ask yourself the following question:

What is the one thing I could achieve that would make today a great day?

After that, you can write down other goals you want to accomplish throughout the day. Always try to work on your most important task first. That alone will make a huge difference. Don't worry too much, though. Just do your best. Sometimes it helps to start your day with a smaller task, or whichever tasks excites you most. This is the way to go on days where you need to build momentum.

Daily Goal-Setting Tip

In this section, you'll find practical tips to help you achieve your goals and develop the right mindset.

Daily Question:

Here you'll find a question related to the topic of the week. Asking yourself questions is a great way to open yourself to new perspectives and to learn more about yourself and what you really want to do in life It'll also be a great opportunity for you to reflect on your life and develop empowering thoughts.

For best results, make sure you take 1 or 2 minutes to genuinely answer the question. You might even want to write it down. The power of putting pen to paper isn't limited to setting goals.

On the 2nd page:

Chores Section

In this section, you'll write down minor tasks and chores you want to get done that day. It's intentionally divided into four sections:

- Appointments/meetings to schedule
- People to contact
- Chores
- Things to purchase

These are generally tasks that take little time.

Tip: You may want to get some of these tasks done when you take breaks between working blocks.

Distraction Crusher

This section is specifically designed to help you overcome procrastination and avoid unnecessary distractions. It will help you improve your focus and strengthen your self-discipline as you train your mind to focus on the task at hand.

You'll be encouraged to write down any insights or ideas you may have as well as anything you remember you need to do. Then, back to work right away. You can always send that quick email or google that word later once you're done with your tasks!

Additional Notes

In this section you can write anything relevant to you

Weekly Review

At the end of each week you'll be able to go over the past 7 days and look at where you succeeded and where you can do better. As a weekly ritual, I suggest you block out 15-30 minutes every Sunday at a specific time to perform your weekly review. As long as you stick to it every week, you'll be good to go.

This section will be a fantastic opportunity for you to reflect on your week and learn as much as you can from it. To do this, you'll ask yourself the following questions:

- What did I do well this week?
- What challenges did I face?
- What did I learn?
- What concrete action will I take next week?

Monthly Review

The monthly review will give us a closer look at the progress you've made throughout the month. It'll be a wonderful opportunity for you to reflect on your progress and identify any challenges, especially regarding your mindset and beliefs.

Be sure to register at the following URL to receive my monthly review videos and other content to help you review your progress.

http://whatispersonaldevelopment.org/planner

As always, feel free to contact me at thibaut.meurisse@gmail.com if you have any questions.

HOW TO SET EXCITING GOALS

Do you already have exciting goals you want to work on? In this section, I'd like to provide you with a powerful method to set goals that are genuinely exciting and in alignment with your values. I'll also help you identify your life purpose. I understand that you may already have a 90-Day goal in mind, but please bear with me and do the exercises. They'll help you gain clarity regarding your goals

Goal-Setting Exercise:

"Setting goals is the first step in turning the invisible into the visible." - Tony Robbins

I'm going to share one of the most powerful goal-setting exercises with you. This exercise is very straightforward; all you have to do is write down every goal you'd like to achieve if you were guaranteed to succeed. Focus on goals that get you excited, even if they sound kind of crazy. What do you want most? What does your dream life look like? How do you want to contribute to the world? Let your imagination run wild!

Whatever you do, don't limit yourself in any way during this exercise. Forget the excuses or limitations for a while and pretend you're playing a game. Make sure you're in a constructive state of mind. You can listen to your favorite music during the exercise or whatever else elevates your mood. Take your time to do the exercise right now, and ask yourself the following question: *What is it I really want?*

You can use the free space below or a separate piece of paper to write down your answer.

This process is crucial. You're unlikely to get much out of this planner if you skip this exercise. So go ahead and give it a try. Don't worry, I'll wait.

All done? Great! How was it? How many inspiring goals did you come up with? How do they make you feel?

Now, here's the funny part. I want you to ask yourself this simple yet powerful question: *How?* How are you going to achieve those big goals? Refrain from using limiting phrases such as "I can't" or "It's impossible". Ban these words and phrases from your vocabulary and try to enjoy yourself as you consider how you'll achieve what you want to accomplish. Take 10 minutes to brainstorm, but focus solely on your most important goal for now. You can always think about the others later and work on them in the future, but let's stick to one for now.

How will you achieve your goals?

Okay, now you've written down your goals and brainstormed about how to achieve the most important one. How did that feel?

Next, I want you to ask yourself, "What's one tiny step I can take today that would bring me closer to that goal?" Keep it in mind. We'll come back to it very soon, but let's have a closer at your core values first.

Is Your Goal in Line with Your Core Values?

"People say you have to have a lot of passion for what you are doing and it's totally true. And the reason is because it's so hard that if you don't, any rational person would give up." - Steve Jobs

It's essential that your goal be in line with your core values. If the goal you're pursuing doesn't sync up with your values and fails to excite you, you're unlikely to achieve it. If you don't have a strong "why" to support your goal, it'll be hard to cope with the obstacles and failures you'll experience along the way to attaining it. You may even find them impossible to endure, which will ultimately cause you to give up.

Identify the Values Behind Your Goals

"Neither pride nor self-esteem can be supported by the pursuit of secondhand values that do not reflect who we really are." – Nathaniel Branden

Understanding the underlying motivations behind your goal will make you feel good about what you wish to achieve. It also provides more reason to persevere when things get tough.

So take your biggest goal and ask yourself why it's so important to you. What are the values you attach to that particular goal? If your goal is to make a certain amount of money, figure out what values you attach to money.

Below is an exercise from hypnotherapist Joseph Clough that will help you identify the values behind your goals and supercharge them. Here's an example of what it will look like upon completion:

What would money bring me?

1. Freedom

a. Time with my family

i. Strong connections

b. Happiness

c. Hobbies

2. Time

a. Hobbies

b. Relaxing activities

c. Working out/Exercising

3. Experiences

a. Travel

b. Excitement

c. Meeting new people

4. Material things

a. A house

i. Comfort

ii. Peacefulness

b. A car

i. Freedom to travel whenever I want

5. Savings

a. Security

b. Treating myself

6. Health

a. Energy

i. More focus

So, what's exciting about your goal? What benefits will you get from achieving it? Complete the exercise below and make your goal as inspiring as you can.

Ex: What would money bring me?	What would your goal get you?

- **Freedom**
   ❯ Time with my family
   ❯ Happiness
   ❯ Hobbies
 	
- **Time**
   ❯ Hobbies
   ❯ Relaxing activities
   ❯ Workouts/running
 	
- **Experiences**
   ❯ Travel
   ❯ Excitement
   ❯ Meeting new people
 	
- **Material things**
   ❯ House
   ❯ Car
 	
- **Savings**
   ❯ Security
   ❯ Treating myself	

Life purpose vs. Ideal Goal

Now that you know your most important goal, you should ask yourself the following question: What is the value of this goal? Remember that a goal is only valuable when the meaning we give it provides us with fulfillment. Your goal is just one of several ways you can achieve the sense of fulfillment you're looking for. As such, it's important to avoid confusing your goal with your life purpose.

For instance, my life purpose is improving myself every day, living up to my full potential, and helping others realize theirs so they can live happier, more fulfilling lives.

For me, realizing my life purpose was transformative. I was shy and passive for most of my life but eventually realized that I wouldn't reach my goals unless I started taking more action. If I stayed as I was, I would reach my deathbed full of regret and knowing I hadn't lived the life I was supposed to nor had the impact that I should have on the world around me.

I didn't want my life to end that way, so I embarked on a journey of personal development that allowed me to come out of my shell slowly but surely. I discovered that I wanted to study, learn, evolve, and improve myself for the rest of my life. I knew that if I could work on myself, become more confident, and take more action, I could help others to do the same.

The main reason I've been able to start a blog, write books, and shoot videos is that these things are in sync with my values and what I want to get out of life. If they didn't motivate me I wouldn't have the courage to follow through, go out of my comfort zone, and keep moving forward despite challenges. Having a life purpose is without a doubt what motivates me to take action.

The idea of unleashing potential is important to me because of those I've watched miss out on their dreams. I have relatives who missed out on so much in life due to lack of confidence, fear of failure, or limiting beliefs. Furthermore, I feel most people greatly underestimate their potential and what they can accomplish in their lives.

My ultimate goal stems from my life purposes and it has three parts. I want to become one of the world's best personal development experts, run a blog with hundreds of thousands of subscribers, and write books that help millions of people unleash their true potential. I could easily be overwhelmed by such an ambitious goal. However, this goal is *not* my life purpose. If my goal is in line with my life purpose, I'll be satisfied even if I fail to achieve that goal. I'll feel fulfilled as long as I have a career that allows me to evolve and help others grow and tap into their potential. There's more than one way to do this, such as coaching or teaching, and these alternatives may or may not involve achieving my ultimate goal.

Identifying the values behind a specific goal like we did in the previous exercise opens us up to new possibilities. It gives us the flexibility to adapt our goals such that they continue to reflect our values. For instance, my original goal was to reach 100,000 page views per month. However, this number had no meaning in itself. What's important is the freedom and sense of accomplishment it would give me. Nowadays, my focus is more on writing, selling more books, and increasing my fan base. Perhaps having a few thousand loyal subscribers or selling several thousand copies-of my book would do it. My short and mid-term goals may have changed slightly, but the nature of my work and the clarity of my vision hasn't.

Now, I'm not saying you should aim lower. In fact, setting an ambitious goal has a lot of benefits. In my specific case, it motivates me to do more and to give as much as I can to my readers, and it can have the same motivational effect on you.

Considering the following questions:

- Have you found your life purpose?
- What are the values behind your biggest goal?
- Why are these values so important to you?
- Are there more effective ways to meet your needs?

Identifying Your Life Purpose

Knowing your core values and having a strong life purpose is vital to enjoying a truly fulfilling life. Unfortunately, many people will spend their lives pursuing the wrong goals because they have no sense of purpose. Most people lack a sense of purpose because they don't really know themselves. They've been trying so hard to meet the expectations of their friends, parents, or society that they haven't learned to listen to themselves. It's difficult to discover your life purpose if you don't know your core values, which is why it's crucial to spend time getting to know yourself. If you want to reach the essence of who you are, you have to eliminate your limiting beliefs and deconstruct the false reality that has been created by your environment.

If your current belief system stems mostly from external influences, you're likely to come up with a life purpose that's clouded by your environment. Keep in mind that you can't accept anything that's out of alignment with your belief system. Therefore, the life purpose you uncover will always reflect your own subjective reality. It may be necessary to change your belief system before you can find your true purpose. As Lao Tzu said, "He who knows others is wise; he who knows himself is enlightened."

Discovering your life purpose will allow you to access your potential, find out what you love, and figure out a way to do it. When this happens, work won't feel like work anymore. As Confucius said, "Choose a job you love, and you will never have to work a day in your life".

Finding your life purpose might take some time. Be patient and learn to listen to your emotions. Figure out what you're passionate about and see what it says about your values. After discovering your true passion, your next step is to commit to it. Make a plan, take action, and persevere. When you do this, it'll be virtually impossible for people or circumstances to stop you!

A great life purpose should be: *

1. **Timeless:** If you could time travel to the past or future, your life purpose would remain the same regardless of the time period.
2. **Universal:** You could have been born in a totally different part of the world and your life purpose would remain the same.
3. **Inspiring:** Your life purpose should be truly inspiring, allow you to unleash your full potential, and create a genuine sense of fulfillment. When you're aligned with your life purpose, the effort you put into it won't feel like work at all.
4. **Transcendent:** Your life purpose should allow you to transcend your ego. Most of us work to survive, gain recognition, accumulate possessions, or feel accepted by society. A genuine life purpose comes from a place of love, not fear. A clear life purpose enables you to stop acting out of fear. Although we may

not be able to eliminate our egos, we should aim to control them and act from a place of love as much as possible.

*from Celestine Chua's e-book *How to Discover Your Life Purpose* (http://personalexcellence.co/free-ebooks/)

Exercises

Exercise 1

Consider the goals you uncovered during the goal-setting exercise and choose the most important one. The goal itself could certainly be a way to express your life purpose. What are the values behind that goal? Take some time to think about these values and try to connect them with a potential life purpose.

Values attached to my goal:

Exercise 2

Ask yourself the following questions:

1. If I had all the money and time in the world, what would I do?
2. What do I love so much that I'd pay to do it?
3. How can I get paid to do it?

Exercise 3

Use a pen and paper to answer the following question: "What is my life purpose?" Don't overthink it; just write whatever comes to mind. Keep doing it until the sentence you've written makes you cry.

This exercise is originally from a Steve Pavlina article. For more information, check out the life purpose section of my bibliography.

The Main Characteristics of Worthy Goals

I believe worthy goals have the following features:

1. They reflect your core values and are what *you* want, not what friends, family, or society may want.
2. They truly excite and energize you.
3. You enjoy the process that leads to them and not just the outcome. "I'll be happy when..." types of goals aren't worth pursuing. Why not be happy now?
4. They involve trying to give rather than get. In other words, you're acting from a place of love rather than fear.

If you want to know whether you're acting out of fear or love, you must closely examine your focus. When you act out of love, you're primarily focused on giving. Acting out of love means that you aren't trying to get people to like you, rather, you just want them to be happy. If you act out of love, the feeling of helping people while doing what you love will make you happy. When you act out of fear, you're focused on receiving something, be it money, approval, recognition, fame, or power. If you get what you want, your main focus will be holding onto it. The desire to be rich, famous, or powerful can certainly motivate people to reach their goals, but that doesn't change the fact that these are fear-based motivations. These sorts of goals are an attempt to use external recognition to fix the emptiness within. These goals aren't simply unworthy of pursuit, they're also a sign of insecurity and low self-esteem, which is why some people who seem successful are deeply unhappy. Money, fame, and other external things may have their perks, but they will never lead to true fulfillment on their own.

So, what do you do if you're motivated by external factors? Start by pondering these three questions: Do you feel you aren't good enough? Are you trying to prove something to yourself or others? What are you trying to achieve with your goal? Acting out of love isn't easy, it takes lots of growth and personal development. It also requires taking stock of your motivations on a regular basis, making a conscious effort to help others, and seeking true fulfillment rather than money or recognition.

Questions to Consider:

Are you acting out of fear?

If so, what does this tell about your self-esteem and the worthiness of your goal?

What can you do about it?

Please note that working on overcoming your fears is one of the most important things you can do for your personal development.

WHAT ARE YOUR GOALS?

By now you should have a specific goal that excites you, something that you'd like to start working on as soon as possible. It might be something you can complete within the coming year, or it might be a long-range goal that takes you several years to achieve.

In the case of bigger goals, it's easy to get discouraged when thinking of all the things you have to do to achieve it. Yet it's important to remember that any goal, no matter how ambitious it is, consists of many steps. These steps can easily be broken down into small tasks you can work on each day. Is it possible for you to focus on one or two small tasks today? I bet you can do it. Can you do it again tomorrow? Sure. This planner is designed to help you do it each and every day until you reap long-term rewards.

Now, I'd like you to get more specific about this thrilling goal. Write it down using the SMART goals methodology. Don't limit yourself, just write what comes to mind.

SMART stands for:

- Specific: What exactly do you want? What are you trying to achieve?

- Measurable: Can you easily assess your progress towards your goal? How will you know if you've achieved it or not?
- Achievable: Is it achievable? Is the timeframe realistic? Can you put in the effort required despite other responsibilities?
- Relevant: Is it in line with your values? Does it excite you?
- Time-bound: Do you have a clear deadline for your goals?

My exciting SMART Goal is:

-

What's Your First Step?

You may not know everything you'll need to do to complete your ultimate goal. It may even seem unrealistic or out of your range, but you probably know what the very first step is. Take some time to think about what that first step is. What could you do today that would build momentum and kick start the process of pursuing your goal?

This first step might entail sending a message to someone, buying a book, or doing some research. Or perhaps it involves calling a friend or going to a particular location. Don't worry about how small the first step might be. Getting started is what matters.

I want you to remember this simple truth: Every goal, regardless of its size, is just a succession of tiny steps taken every day. The more you break your goal into manageable tasks, the easier it'll be to achieve it. By taking small but daily steps, you'll build the kind of momentum that fuels action. Goals that once seemed impossible will start looking obtainable. You'll also avoid the unpleasant pressure that comes from dealing with huge goals. This, in turn, will reduce the potential for self-sabotage.

Write down your first step below:

My first step is:

Now it's time to look at your goal. What can you reasonably achieve in 90 days? This is a question that only *you* can answer. Let's say you want to write and publish your first book. How far can you get in 90 days? Can you write the first chapter or complete the first draft? Can you complete the entire book and have it published?

I'd like you to pay close attention to your body and your emotions when you answer this question. I encourage you to say your goal out loud. How does that make you feel? Do you believe you can achieve it? It's imperative to set a 90-Day Goal that you genuinely believe to be possible. Ideally, your confidence level should be 8 or higher on a scale of 1 to 10. Your goal should feel like a bit of a stretch, but doable nonetheless. Don't worry too much, though. It doesn't have to be perfect, just follow your intuition for now. You can always adjust your goal at the end of the 90-day period. You might, for instance, come to find that you can achieve your goal faster than you originally thought. On the other hand, you might find that your goal was a little bit too ambitious, in which case you could scale it down for the time being.

So go ahead and write down your 90-Day Goal using the SMART methodology. It's an important goal, and you'll be thinking about it as often as possible for the next 90 days. With this planner, you'll be able to turn thoughts into daily actions that bring your closer to your goal.

My 90-Day Goal is:

Reverse Engineering Your Goal

Now we're going to reverse engineer your goal. Just ask yourself what you could reasonably achieve in 30 days and record your answer. As before, use the SMART goal methodology to write it down.

What I can achieve in the next 30 days:

Committing to Your Goal

Most people never fully commit to anything, and this is usually one of the biggest problems in their lives. Many start something but grow too bored to finish it. Others maintain their interest but become so frustrated by lack of results that they abandon it and jump to the next thing that pops up. I don't want that to happen to you, which is why I want you to become fully dedicated to your 90-Day Goal. Committing doesn't have to take time. In fact, it can be done in a matter of seconds. When you commit to something, it creates a feeling that generates a certain type of energy. This energy is the very essence of commitment! Use it as fuel to work on your goal for the next 90 days. If you're not fond of commitment, you're not alone. Just keep in mind this is a short-term commitment. You can always do something else after the 90 days are up, so there's no need to feel anxious or trapped.

Once you've devoted yourself to your goal, I'd like you to sign a pledge to further cement your commitment.

Your 90-Day Goal Pledge

I hereby declare that I will set daily goals that will bring me closer to achieving my 90-Day Goal. I will take action towards these goals every day, no matter how small that action may be. By doing so, I'll slowly but steadily move closer to my goals with each passing day.

Regardless of the results, I commit to maintaining consistency and going through the goal-setting process on a daily basis.

I will continually work on my 90-Day Goal, which is:

-

I will avoid the following:

Getting discouraged by lack of results. I will instead focus primarily on the process, because I understand that my daily actions are what really counts.

Chasing new opportunities that distract me from my main goal. I will instead refocus the moment I notice myself getting off track.

Giving up due to self-sabotage, self-criticism, or negative thoughts. I will instead remind myself that these are just the byproducts of my mind's resistance to change.

Your name:

Today's date:

HOW TO SET DAILY GOALS

At this point, you've got a goal that you can't wait to start working on. In this section, we're going to discuss the process of setting daily goals that will support your 90-Day Goal.

The Power of Pen and Paper

You should always set your daily goals in writing. There's something magical in getting your goals on paper. It's as if what you've been daydreaming about suddenly becomes part of the physical world. When you're in need of clarity or have a problem to solve, writing down your thoughts, feelings, and ideas is one of the best things you can do.

Formulating Your Daily Goals for Optimal Effectiveness

Great daily goals have many characteristics, but the following list details some of the most important ones.

Great daily goals are:

1. **Prioritized** – You work on your most important goal first. Typically, this is the goal that scares you the most or that you'd prefer to put last on your list.
2. **As specific as possible** - You know exactly what needs to be

done and can easily measure whether you've successfully completed your task.

3. **Clearly actionable** – They're stated using full sentences with subjects that include specific action verbs.
4. **Stated in a positive way** – You can use "I will..." rather than "I won't" statements.
5. **Easy to envision** – You can easily visualize yourself completing each task before you do it.
6. **Easy to clarify**- You can confirm whether or not you're clear about what needs to be done. Go through each task twice and ask yourself precisely what it entails. Be sure to say your answer out loud each time. If you can do this with ease, you're on the right track.

The following questions can further assist you in this process:

- What one thing could I do that would make today a great day?
- What task am I least interested in doing? What task am I most scared of? As mentioned before, this is usually the first thing you should do.
- Will continuing to do what I'm doing today result in accomplishing my goals?

I filled in a template to help you set your daily goals. This template will give you an idea of what daily goal-setting looks like.

Daily quote

People without goals are doomed to work forever for people who do have goals. - Brian Tracy

Daily goals:

1. I'll easily *shoot a 2 to 3-minute video and upload it to YouTube.
2. I'll easily create the first draft of chapters 3 and 4 of my goal-setting planner.
3. I'll easily complete my article "11 Signs You Might Change the World" and send it to my editor.

the underlined words are action verbs. What do I need to do, exactly? **Shoot, upload, create, complete, and send.**

Daily tips: The "If 1 then 1 million" rule.

Example 1: If I can sell one book, then I can sell a million.

The reasoning: If one person likes my book, there have to be dozens, hundreds, thousands, or maybe even millions of others who will like it, too. It's my job to find them.

Example 2: If I can make $1 online, I can make $1,000,000.

The reasoning: If I could find a way to make $1 online, I just have to repeat the process, continually scaling up each time.

Example 3: If I find one client, I can find thousands more.

The reasoning: If I was able to attract one client to my business then there are dozens or even hundreds more that would be interested in my services.

Empowering question:

Why will I achieve my goals?

Meetings/Appointments	People to contact
- 5pm: See the dentist	- Send email to John - Call Brian
Chores	**Things to purchase**
- Go to the post office	- Buy gift to Jeremy

Distraction crusher

- Send email to X.
- Write articles about Y.
- Look for information regarding Z.

Additional notes (insights, lessons learned etc.)

HOW TO WORK ON YOUR GOALS EFFECTIVELY

Now that you've set our goals, you're probably wondering how to ensure you're working on them properly. In this section, we'll mention briefly how you can increase productivity, maximize efficiency, and overcome procrastination by giving 3 secrets to beat procrastination. To learn in more details about procrastination you can refer to Lesson 7 "Beating procrastination and supercharging your productivity"

3 Secrets to Stay Focused and Beat Procrastination

1. Eliminate Distractions.

Start by minimizing the potential for distractions since virtually any distraction can become tempting when the urge to procrastinate strikes. Here's what you can do to get rid of them:

A. Use a time log to find any "procrastination patterns". Record everything you do throughout the day. Where are you wasting time? Why? How much is due to procrastination?

B. Create a Not-To-Do List based on the time log results. Put the list on your desk so you can see it easily. (ex: Don't check emails, don't go on YouTube etc.)

The next line of defense is removing all distractions from your desk. You should also plan your tasks in advance, prepare your environment, and give yourself a way to jot down intrusive thoughts.

The day before you start working on your task, you can also spend some time visualizing yourself doing it. This will help you condition your mind and decrease the risk of distractions.

2. Become Aware of Your Fears and Emotions.

It's essential to get in touch with the feelings that come up when you're about to start working on an important task. What is that feeling that makes you want to procrastinate and escape? Stay with that feeling. Face it. Look at it closely. It's nothing more than your mind trying to trick you. See how that works? Becoming aware of your feelings will reduce the likelihood you procrastinate.

3. Reduce the Friction Associated with Starting the Task

It's crucial to reduce the discomfort involved in beginning your task. You can accomplish this through visualization. Consider your current feelings and imagine how you'll feel once your task is completed. If that doesn't work, just start and see what happens. Tell yourself you'll only work on it for five minutes. You can do almost anything for five minutes, right?

My Weekly Goals

Your ONE habit

Are you ready to start working on your goal? This week we're going to establish that ONE habit that will help you achieve it. Goals are much easier to achieve once you have daily habits that fully support them.

So, what is the one daily habit that would contribute most to attaining your goal? Write it down below:

My ONE Daily Habit

This is the one habit you'll stick to every day this week (and likely beyond) until you reach your goal.

-

My 3 Core Tasks

These are your most important tasks of the week. They all relate to your 90-Day Goal, and you'll do whatever it takes to achieve them this week.

-

-

-

Other tasks to accomplish (may or may not be related to your goal)

-

-

-

-

LESSON 1

OVERCOMING VICTIM MENTALITY

How often do you play the victim? Tony Robbins likes to say that the only distance between you and your goals is the story you're telling yourself. For some reason, we as people love to play the victim. Sometimes we derive a sort of twisted pleasure from it, don't we?

Playing the victim is very convenient. It allows you to make excuses about why you aren't pursuing your dreams or doing what you know you should. It also gives you some fantastic reasons to avoid the following:

- Taking action
- Facing your fears
- Getting out of your comfort zone
- Experiencing repeated failures
- Being laughed at
- Being told that it can't be done
- Being rejected
- Having your ego crushed
- Working hard
- Looking at yourself in the mirror and realize you need to make changes

This is just a small sampling of the myriad of things Victim Mentality excuses you from.

Avoiding these things may sound appealing on paper. We don't have infinite time, however. What seems safe and secure now can turn into cause for regret and sadness as you get older, and utter despair as you near the end of your life.

I really want to support you in overcoming the impulse to play the victim. Almost all of us do it, and for those of us who don't currently do it, it's likely that we have in the past. The willingness to take full responsibility for yourself is what will allow you to make drastic changes in your life. After all, you can't change something you don't feel some measure of responsibility for.

What I'm saying here might sound harsh, so I want to clarify something that's frequently misunderstood. You might not like being told to drop your excuses or to stop playing the victim. You might get defensive or feel as if you aren't being heard or respected. Many people feel this way, and it's perfectly understandable.

That said, I'm not trying to take away from the fact that you have probably faced difficult situations that were completely beyond your control. We all face many challenges in life and they aren't going to disappear any time soon. When I talk about the importance of dropping your excuses, I'm not suggesting you deny your challenges. Your challenges are real. Your pain, be it physical or mental, is real. Your lack of time, money, or resources is part of your reality at the moment.

Dropping your excuses simply means that, after fully acknowledging your problems, you accept them and move forward. You don't let them drag you down, and you give yourself permission to achieve your goals in spite of them. Dropping your excuses and giving up victimhood just means recognizing that you're bigger than your problems. They don't have to stop you from being successful.

The world has seen its fair share of people who have overcome tremendous challenges to accomplish extraordinary feats. Many of these people were poor, lacked formal education, had no special talents, and were of average intelligence.

There is something that they did have, however, and it's a prerequisite to achieving your goals and dreams. That thing is **resourcefulness**. Once you have that, you can find all sorts of ways to obtain the necessary resources to get from where you are to where you want to be. If you can't find a way to access these resources, you can find a way to work around their absence. In short, you'll be able to work through challenges and get what you want with or without them.

Take a look at these examples of resourcefulness:

- Outstanding self-discipline
- Unshakable faith in yourself
- An extremely powerful vision
- An insane work ethic
- The ability to maintain absolute commitment to your goals from start to finish
- High levels of self-awareness
- A genuine desire to positively impact as many lives as possible
- Sincere compassion for other human beings
- The ability to persevere no matter how hard things get
- The ability to inspire others with what you write or say
- Complete clarity about what you want in life
- Consistency that persists day after day and year after year
- An obsessive desire to learn and become better each day
- The capacity to reflect and learn from your mistakes
- The courage to get out of your comfort zone
- The boldness to push past fears and make your move

Wouldn't these things be a big help when it comes to making your dreams come true?

The good news is that everything in this list is a skill, which means they can all be learned or even mastered. Don't worry if this list seems overwhelming. While each skill is extremely helpful, you don't have to master them all to live the life you want.

Keep in mind how far ahead of the game you already are. Most people don't set any sort of goals, to say nothing of setting them daily and using a planner. According to Brian Tracy, a personal development expert who has taught millions of people to set goals, only 3% of the population has clear written goals. Unsurprisingly, these are usually the people who end up being the most successful.

Of course, I don't want you to stop at setting goals, I want you to achieve them as well! I hope that daily use of this planner will help you develop the mindset needed to achieve your biggest goals.

Remember, you don't need more resources such as money, connections, or formal education. You don't have to be a genius. Resources can certainly help, but they are by no means a necessity. If you become more resourceful, you'll be able to get everything you need to get where you want to go. What you lack in resources can be made up for in the skills you choose to develop.

Now that you know how important resourcefulness is, think about the skills you'd like to learn. What is the one skill that, if mastered, would best help you achieve your goal?

Day 1

Date: _____

> *Take your life in your own hands, and what happens? A terrible thing:*
> *no one to blame*

— ERICA JONG

Daily goals:

-

-

-

-

-

-

Daily tip: *Real difficulties? YES. Excuses? NO!*

As Tony Robbins says, "The only people without problems are those in cemeteries." We all have problems and challenges. I've been in situations that were painful, difficult, or just plain unfair, and I'm sure you have, too. Never forget what dropping your excuses truly means. It doesn't mean your problems are imaginary or that you should pretend they don't exist. They're real and could potentially stop you from reaching your goals, but they don't have to. You can make the choice to commit yourself to achieving your goals **despite** the very real challenges in your life.

Empowering question

If you took full responsibility for your life, what would you do differently?

Meetings/Appointments	People to contact
Chores	Things to purchase

Distraction crusher

Additional notes (insights, lessons learned etc.)

Day 2

Date: _____

> *The victim mindset dilutes the human potential. By not accepting personal responsibility for our circumstances, we greatly reduce our power to change them.*

— STEVE MARABOLI

Daily goals:

-
-
-
-
-
-

Daily tip: *What's your excuse?*

Ask yourself what has kept you from achieving your goals? Your biggest excuses will be the first things that come to mind. You might say, "I don't have time", "I don't have money", "I don't know the right people", or something along those lines. I want to challenge you on that. Come up with 10 ideas to achieve your goals and write them down. What's the one idea you can start working on immediately?

Empowering question

What is one thing you could take responsibility for right now instead of blaming other people or external circumstances?

Meetings/Appointments	People to contact
Chores	Things to purchase

Distraction crusher

Additional notes (insights, lessons learned etc.)

Day 3

Date: _____

> *I do not believe in excuses. I believe in hard work as the prime solvent of life's problems.*

— JAMES CASH PENNEY

Daily goals

-

-

-

-

-

Daily tip: *Stop thinking that you have more problems than other people.*

We often think other people have it easier than us, but is it really true? While some people might have relatively easily lives, there are a whole lot of people who don't. In many cases, they have problems that you simply can't see.

They may be sick, depressed, or in pain. They may be struggling with emotional scars from childhood. They could be in a toxic relationship. They may have experienced violence or some other type of abuse. Or maybe they're being harassed at work. Who knows what they've been through or are currently going through. The thing is, it doesn't even matter whether your problems are bigger than those of the people around you. Even if they are, it doesn't change anything about your situation. As such, it's always better to assume other people have it as hard as you do and refuse to play the victim.

Empowering question

Do you think you have more problems than others? How has this belief served you?

Meetings/Appointments	People to contact
Chores	Things to purchase

Distraction crusher

Additional notes (insights, lessons learned etc.)

Day 4

Date: _____

> *People spend too much time finding other people to blame, too much energy finding excuses for not being what they are capable of being, and not enough energy putting themselves on the line, growing out of the past, and getting on with their lives.*

— J. MICHAEL STRACZYNSKI

Daily goals

-
-
-
-
-
-

Daily tip: *Don't be selfish.*

Are you being the best you can be? Self-improvement is key to being able to make a positive impact on the world. With that in mind, isn't it somewhat selfish to neglect your self-growth? How many people could you help if you stopped making excuses and started doing what you know you should? The choice is yours to make, but I firmly believe that breaking free of self-imposed limitations will make the world a better place. It needs more people who are willing to take responsibility for their lives and go after their dreams.

Empowering question

If you had no fear of failure or rejection, how many people's lives could you impact with your gifts, talents, or passions?

Meetings/Appointments	People to contact
Chores	Things to purchase

Distraction crusher

Additional notes (insights, lessons learned etc.)

Day 5

Date: _____

As long as you think that the cause of your problem is 'out there'—as long as you think that anyone or anything is responsible for your suffering—the situation is hopeless. It means that you are forever in the role of victim, that you're suffering in paradise.

— Byron Katie

Daily goals

-

-

-

-

-

-

Daily tip: *You can't set goals without taking responsibility for your life.*

Taking full responsibility in all areas of life is extremely important. Your goals are here to help you take control of your life. But you can't set them if you don't believe you're responsible for your life in the first place. How can you set financial goals if you don't believe you have the power to improve your finances? How can you change your mindset if you don't believe you can control your thoughts? So take full responsibility for your life and see what happens. You'll definitely see some major changes coming in your way!

Empowering question

How do you feel when I say you should take full responsibility for your life? Do you get defensive? If so, why?

Meetings/Appointments	People to contact
Chores	Things to purchase

Distraction crusher

Additional notes (insights, lessons learned etc.)

Day 6

Date: _____

Excuses change nothing, but make everyone feel better.

— MASON COOLEY

Daily goals

-

-

-

-

-

-

Daily tip: *Dare to look in the mirror.*

Excuses are merely distractions we use to avoid looking in the mirror. It's easier to make excuses than to accept our mistakes, insecurities, or fears. Yet it's the ability to be brutally honest with yourself that leads to the greatest amount of growth. You can't, however, allow this honesty to lead to self-pity, which ultimately becomes an excuse to give up. What about you? Will you dare to take a look in the mirror?

Empowering question

How do your excuses make you feel better about yourself and how do they hold you back?

Meetings/Appointments	People to contact
Chores	Things to purchase

Distraction crusher

Additional notes (insights, lessons learned etc.)

Day 7

Date: _____

He that is good for making excuses is seldom good for anything else.

— BENJAMIN FRANKLIN

Daily goals

-

-

-

-

-

-

Daily tip: *Make the time.*

If your favorite excuse is "I don't have time", then I have something for you. From now on, whenever you catch yourself saying "I don't have time" add "because X isn't a priority" or "because X isn't important to me". See how it feels to add those words. Consider the following phrases:

- I don't have time to go to the doctor because my health isn't a priority.
- I don't have time to work on my business after work because becoming financially free and living from my passion doesn't matter to me.
- I don't have time to have dinner with my family because my family isn't important to me".

How did it feel when you read these phrases? Are you sure you don't have time?

Empowering question

What changes can you make to free up time for what matters to you?

Meetings/Appointments	People to contact
Chores	Things to purchase

Distraction crusher

Additional notes (insights, lessons learned etc.)

STORY OF THE WEEK

Stefan Pylarinos – *Take action! Take action! Take action!*

"But when you have the regret and you didn't follow through, you didn't give it all, you didn't take action. That is the ultimate pain when it comes to the end of your life." – Stefan Pylarinos

Stefan Pylarinos is an online entrepreneur and founder of *www.projectlifemastery.com*. He's a great example of how powerful setting goals can be. He's a huge advocate of having clear, specific goals, and he has a lot to show for it. His impressive track record includes an online business that generates 7 figures per year. He's primarily focused on helping others improve their lives and create online businesses.

Pylarinos created his website in 2012 and began preparing for a fitness competition in 2013. He started sharing his goals on his website to create accountability during the preparation process. The benefits he experienced from doing this are what convinced him to share them on a monthly basis. He has been posting video updates regarding his goals since 2014.

Though setting clear goals isn't the only reason for his success, I'm betting he would agree that goal-setting has been a contributing factor to it. He uses both his website and YouTube videos to share fantastic tips that will help you set and achieve your goals.

Weekly Goal Review - week 1

Congratulations! You've made it to the end of the first week. You're well on your way to achieving your goal and mastering the goal-setting process.

Now it's time to review your progress and get ready for next week.

What challenges did you face this week?

What beliefs are interfering with your ability to reach your goals? Is there a mindset that's making it harder to achieve them? Come up with at least one or two beliefs, even if they aren't having a negative impact on you right now. They still have the potential to sabotage your efforts, and that's all that matters.

Example: "I'm not good enough", "I focus too much on results", "I get discouraged easily", "I don't have enough discipline", "I can't motivate myself", or "I procrastinate". These are just some of many limiting beliefs and negative mindsets that people struggle with.

-

-

-

What could you do next week that would help you overcome your limiting beliefs?

Example:

- I'm not good enough → I'll spend 5 minutes journaling about my accomplishments and things I'm grateful for. I'll continually look for ways to add new entries to my journal.
- I get discouraged because I don't get any results → I'll spend 2 to 3 minutes every morning reminding myself to focus on the process. I'll continually remind myself that it's what I do every day that matters. I'll take time at the end of the day to congratulate myself for taking action regardless of the results.

My Weekly Goals

My ONE Daily Habit

This is the one habit you'll stick to every day this week (and likely beyond) until you reach your goal.

-

My 3 Core Tasks

These are your most important tasks of the week. They all relate to your 90-Day Goal, and you'll do whatever it takes to achieve them this week.

-

-

-

Other tasks to accomplish (may or may not be related to your goal)

-

-

-

-

-

-

-

LESSON 2

BREAKING FREE OF SOCIAL CONDITIONING AND CREATING
UNSHAKABLE BELIEFS

Be realistic! How often have you heard those two words? Or perhaps you're the one saying them. Unfortunately, you've been conditioned since birth to believe that the world is divided into two things: what you can do, and what you can't (or shouldn't) do. Society has convinced you that it's okay to be average, and has placed its own standards upon you. These standards apply to everything from work ethic, self-discipline, and self-esteem to integrity, the amount of money you should earn, and how big your dreams should be. Is meeting these standards the best you can do? Of course not! If you start doing something just a little bit differently, the people around you try to pull you back to "reality". In any society, there's a massive gravitational pull towards mediocrity, because it's what allows most people to "fit in".

Too many of your assumptions go unchallenged. Society tells you that you should work 40+ years in a cubicle and retire at 65. Why? Is that the only option? Is there nothing else you can do? Society tries to tell you what to watch, what to talk about, how to behave, what to buy, and even what to think.

I'm more interested in what *you* can do than in what your family and friends *believe* you can do. I'm more interested in seeing you become the best person you can be rather than what society expects you to be. Life is fascinating as it gives us enormous room for growth. As I mentioned in the last lesson, we can develop and master any skill we need in life.

Your main job is to become crystal clear about what you want to accomplish in life and devote yourself to becoming the person you need to be to achieve the compelling vision you have for yourself. Jim Rohn put it beautifully when he said, "The major reason for setting a goal is for what it makes of you to accomplish it. What it makes of you will always be the far greater value than what you get."

Society is, to a large extent, preventing you from living up to your potential. It certainly doesn't provide you with the powerful and unshakable beliefs you must hold to get the results you want in life. Read on for some examples of what I mean by this.

1. Failure is perceived as a negative occurrence that should be feared.

Failure has a bad reputation. We didn't learn about the value of failure in school. Nobody told us that the ability to learn from our mistakes (and accept the inevitability of making mistakes) is one of the most powerful skills there is. I see so many people who don't bother trying anything because they're afraid to fail. But remember this: You'll learn far more from trying and failing than by doing nothing at all. Would you rather play it safe and accomplish nothing or experience failure on your way to success?

2. The standard for self-discipline is low.

What we generally think of as self-discipline isn't actually self-discipline, especially if you consider what our minds are truly capable of. Wim Hof successfully runs marathons in freezing temperatures while wearing little more than a pair of shorts. In Japan, the Marathon Monks of Mount Hiei walk the equivalent of a marathon every day in the mountains with only sandals to protect their feet. After this, they manage heavy duty cleaning when they return to the temple at night. These are extreme examples, but they illustrate the following point: The vast majority of us can accomplish much, much more than we think we can. Don't get fooled by what most people call self-discipline. It pales in comparison to what you're actually capable of.

3. No one talks about what it takes to be successful.

Because you don't know what to expect when starting a business, trying to lose weight, or making any other major changes in your life, you give up too easily. If you had a better understanding of the amount of work it takes, it would be a totally different story. You'd be prepared for the obstacles and setbacks. And you would view them as normal, rather than as something that warrants giving up. Let's be honest. Most people's definition of hard work isn't actually hard work. It is for this reason that they end up failing, at which point they tend to blame themselves. They say they aren't smart enough to complete their goal, or point to some other deficiency that has nothing to do with their failure.

I can't tell you how many times I've seen people give up on something they've barely started. More often than not, they start making excuse after excuse: "I'm too old", "I'm not smart enough", "I don't have time", and so on.

A good example of this is when people tell me what a genius I am because I'm fluent in Japanese while they struggle to learn English. I never fail to remind them that I've spent more than 10,000 hours studying Japanese (if not 20,000 hours!) and that I'm not as good as I should be when you consider how much time I've devoted to it. Does this motivate them to study harder? No.

To make matters worse, our world is full of get-rich-quick schemes, crash diets, and other things that promise fast results. It's much easier for companies to make money by promoting products that deliver instant results. According to them, their products will help you lose weight in in record time with very little effort. This further fuels the unhealthy "things should be easy" mentality that is so rampant in the world. This mindset is very damaging, because it gives us unrealistic expectations and sets us up for frustration.

This week provides a great opportunity for you to reconsider your current set of beliefs and start building more empowering ones. These new beliefs will support your quest to become the best you can be.

What about you? Has society led you to believe things should be easier than they are?

Remember Will Smith words: "being realistic is the most commonly traveled road to mediocrity. Why would you be realistic? What's the point of being realistic?"

Day 8

Date: _____

The fishing is best where the fewest go, and the collective insecurity of the world makes it easy for people to hit home runs while everyone else is aiming for base hits. There is just less competition for bigger goals. If you are insecure, guess what? The rest of the world is, too. Do not overestimate the competition and underestimate yourself. You are better than you think.

— TIMOTHY FERRISS

Daily goals

-

-

-

-

-

-

Daily tip: *Why would you want to be realistic?*

What I believe I can do is likely different from what you think you can do because we have different visions of the world based on our own distinct belief systems. What people around you define as realistic isn't your business and shouldn't concern you. Only YOU can decide what's realistic for you! Be careful, though. When you define something as unrealistic, you remove any and all possibilities to make it happen.

Empowering question

What would you seek to achieve if you were guaranteed to succeed at everything you do?

Meetings/Appointments	People to contact
Chores	Things to purchase

Distraction crusher

Additional notes (insights, lessons learned etc.)

Day 9

Date: _____

Whether you think you can or you think you can't, you're right.

— Henry Ford

Day goals

-

-

-

-

-

-

Daily tip: *If he can, I can.*

I really like thinking about this phrase. Contrary to what most people believe, the human brain is not that different from one person to another. If somebody else can do it, you probably can, too. Is there anything someone else is doing that you don't believe you can do? Is this belief accurate? Take a minute to come up with the reasons you can do it!

Empowering question

What are some of the reasons you'll achieve your goals?

Meetings/Appointments	People to contact
Chores	Things to purchase

Distraction crusher

Additional notes (insights, lessons learned etc.)

Day 10

Date: _____

The value of goals is not in the future they describe, but the change in perception of reality they foster.

— David Allen

Daily goals

-

-

-

-

-

-

Daily tip: *Be the kind of person who attracts success.*

Jim Rohn said it best when he stated that, "Success is not to be pursued. It is to be attracted by the person you become. To shift your focus, ask yourself the following question: Who do I need to become to achieve my goals? What are the beliefs, mindsets, and behaviors of people who have what I want? Now, make an effort to work on closing the gap by developing the mindset, skills, and beliefs you need to become that person.

Empowering question

Visualize life after achieving your primary goal. How does future you think, feel, and act?

Meetings/Appointments	People to contact
Chores	Things to purchase

Distraction crusher

Additional notes (insights, lessons learned etc.)

Day 11

Date: _____

If you don't design your own life plan, chances are you'll fall into someone else's plan. And guess what they have planned for you? Not much.

— JIM ROHN

Day goals

-

-

-

-

-

-

Daily tips: *You're the only one who can design your life.*

No one is going to design your life for you, and if they do, it certainly won't be the life YOU desire. If there's something you'd like to see happen in your life, you have to get out there and start taking action on a daily basis. You have to keep going until your vision gives way to tangible, real-life results.

Empowering question

The life you want for yourself is often different than the one others want for you. So which one are you living?

Meetings/Appointments	People to contact
Chores	Things to purchase

Distraction crusher

Additional notes (insights, lessons learned etc.)

Day 12

Date: _____

I've never really viewed myself as particularly talented, where I excel is ridiculous, sickening work ethic. You know while the other guy's sleeping. I'm working, while the other guy's eating, I'm working.

— WILL SMITH

Day goals

-

-

-

-

-

-

Daily tips: *There's nothing wrong with working hard.*

Whatever you want to accomplish in life, you'll need to work hard for it. If you don't, you'll wind up stuck in an unfulfilling job and living an equally unfulfilling life. Only you can decide the sacrifices you're willing to make to achieve your goals. Can you reduce the amount of time you spend watching TV? Can you cut back on video games? This may be hard to believe, but a 2016 study revealed that the average American watches roughly five hours of television per day. That's 1,825 hours per year! Don't you think you could achieve your goals faster if you spent 1,825 hours a year working on them?

Empowering question

What is one simple thing you can do right now to create a more empowering environment for yourself?

Meetings/Appointments	People to contact
Chores	Things to purchase

Distraction crusher

Additional notes (insights, lessons learned etc.)

Day 13

Date: _____

We will act consistently with our view of who we truly are, whether that view is accurate or not.

— TONY ROBBINS

Daily goals

-

-

-

-

-

-

Daily tip: *Your reality isn't reality.*

What you believe you can (or can't) do isn't based on reality. It's just a reflection of what you've been told since childhood. In fact, many of your current beliefs have gone completely unchallenged, which has led to slew of self-imposed limitations. It's important to see them for what they really are if you want to break free from them. These limitations are merely beliefs. Beliefs aren't reality, so why not choose some that are more empowering?

Empowering question

What belief could you start developing today that would make a big difference in your life?

Meetings/Appointments	People to contact
Chores	Things to purchase

Distraction crusher

Additional notes (insights, lessons learned etc.)

Day 14

Date: _____

If you want to be successful, find someone who has achieved the results you want and copy what they do and you'll achieve the same results.

— TONY ROBBINS

Daily goals

-

-

-

-

-

-

Daily tip: *Stop reinventing the wheel.*

Your goal has been accomplished by many other people, virtually none of whom are any smarter or more talented than you. As such, all you have to do is copy what they did. Train yourself to think like they do and adopt their daily habits until you reach your goal. You don't need to be extraordinarily creative to achieve success. A touch of creativity is never a bad thing, but keep in mind that it's those with decades of experience that will be able to come up with something genuinely new in your area of interest. Most people repackage old things by adding their own personal flair to something that's been done before, and there's nothing wrong with that. Don't reinvent the wheel. Instead, use proven methods and keep persevering until you achieve your goal.

Empowering question

What could you do to minimize your learning curve and reach your goal faster?

Meetings/Appointments	People to contact
Chores	Things to purchase

Distraction crusher

Additional notes (insights, lessons learned etc.)

STORY OF THE WEEK

Tony Robbins – *Raise your standards*

"Setting goals is the first step in turning the invisible into the visible." – Tony Robbins

Tony Robbins is arguably one of the most prominent figures in personal development today. He's also a great example of someone who achieved exceptional results by combining the power of goal setting with massive action. He references this in the following excerpt of his popular book *Awaken The Giant Within*:

"Eight years ago, in 1983, I did an exercise that created a future so compelling that my whole life changed as a result. As part of the overall process of raising my standards, I established a whole new set of goals, writing down all the things I would no longer settle for, as well as what I was committed to having in my life. I set aside all my limiting beliefs and sat down on the beach with my journal."

When he set his goals he didn't think in terms of whether they were realistic. Instead, he went after goals that genuinely inspired him.

"I wrote continuously for three hours, brainstorming every possibility of what I could ever imagine doing, being, having, creating, experiencing, or contributing. The timeline I gave myself for achieving these goals was any time

from tomorrow to the next twenty years. I never stopped to think whether I could actually achieve these goals or not. I simply captured any possibility that inspired me, and wrote it down."

Another interesting point is that he focused not only on short-term and mid-term goals, but also on very long-term goals that he wanted to achieve decades later.

Tony Robbins balanced short-term "realistic" goals with a compelling, long-term vision that was big enough to seem impossible. Doing this enabled him to tap into what seems like an infinite amount of motivation and achieve extraordinary things in his life.

Tony's example also highlights the power of clarity, which, as he says, is power in and of itself.

"On that day, I set specific goals that transformed my life. I described the woman of my dreams, detailing what she would be like mentally, emotionally, physically, spiritually. I described what my kids would be like, the huge income that I would enjoy, and the home that I would live in, including the third-story circular office area that would overlook the ocean.

A year and a half later, Life magazine was in my home, interviewing me as to how I had made such incredible shifts in my life. When I pulled out my map to show them all the goals I had written down, it was amazing to see how many I'd achieved. I had met the woman I described down to the finest detail, including the third-story office in the turret of the castle, overlooking the ocean. When I wrote them down initially, I had no assurances whatsoever that these goals could be achieved. But I had been willing to suspend judgment for a short period of time in order to make it work."

While we may not be able to replicate Tony Robbins' extraordinary results in our own lives, the conclusion we can draw from his story is that nobody has ever achieved incredible goals without a strong commitment, a clear and compelling vision, and a specific plan of action.

What is your vision? How do you plan to get there?

Weekly Goal Review - week 2

Congratulations! You've made it to the end of the second week. Way to go!

Don't you feel like you're starting to break free from social conditioning, even just a little bit?

It's now time to review your progress.

Use the space below to write down what went well this week:

Now, write down what you could have done better:

Last week you recorded some beliefs that prevent you from achieving your goals. Have you seen any progress? Use the space below to jot down what went well and what you could have done better.

What went well:

What I could have done better:

Lastly, use the space below to write any new limiting beliefs you may have discovered and what you'll do to overcome them.

My Weekly Goals

My ONE Daily Habit

This is the one habit you'll stick to every day this week (and likely beyond) until you reach your goal.

-

My 3 Core Tasks

These are your most important tasks of the week. They all relate to your 90-Day Goal, and you'll do whatever it takes to achieve them this week.

-

-

-

Other tasks to accomplish (may or may not be related to your goal)

-

-

-

-

-

-

-

LESSON 3

WORKING WITH HARSH REALITIES

Have you given up on a goal in the past? If so, why? One of the biggest mistakes people make when setting goals is inaccurately assessing the amount of time and effort necessary to achieve them. Most of us tend to underestimate the amount of work our goals will take. This underestimation is often severe, and a far cry from how much work is actually needed. In this week's lesson, I'd like to help you get in touch with what it will really take to achieve your goals. I refer to this as a harsh reality, although it won't seem so bad once you adjust to it. When you learn to accept it, you'll realize that it doesn't have to kill your dreams.

The ability to persevere is directly linked to your expectations regarding the amount of work it takes to achieve your goal. If you underestimate it, it won't be long before you feel frustrated and deficient due to lack of results. Worse still, you'll start to resent people who do get them. All this because you never fully realized the amount of work you had ahead of you.

Many of us are overly optimistic when planning things, which is why a number of projects are finished late, go over their budget, or both. The harsh reality is this: Whenever you set a goal, there are a lot of things that can go wrong. In many cases, they *will* go wrong, and you may have to lower your expectations repeatedly. You're bound to run into technical difficulties, people problems, health issues, dips in motivation, self-doubt, disappointments, or something of the like. However, none of these issues can stop you in and of themselves; it's only your reaction to them that will make the difference between success and failure. For most people, reacting poorly to setbacks will lead to failure, but you don't have to be one of those people.

These roadblocks don't pop up because you're unlucky, aren't good enough, lack intelligence, or are in some way incompetent. Nor are they signs that you should give up. Do you remember the victim mentality I discussed in the first chapter? It's often triggered by setbacks, but you have to fight it. These issues happen to all of us, and those who persevere and move past them tend to become the most successful. Now, let's go over some tips that will help you press on in the face of obstacles.

What's the worst that could happen?

It's crucial to think about what could go wrong during the journey towards your goal. This mental preparation will go a long way when it comes to sticking to your goal in spite of challenges.

So what's the ultimate worst-case scenario for you? It might be discovering that your friends and relatives aren't supportive of your goals. It could be losing a lot of money and having to start from scratch. Or maybe your worst-case scenario entails everything going wrong for the first few months. There are many things that might happen as you work towards your goal, so take the time to play around with this idea and visualize some of the craziest scenarios you can think of. The question is, what would you do if these scenarios were to happen? Refer to the section on "My Pledge to Becoming Unstoppable" at the end of this planner to learn more about handling challenging times.

What would make you give up on your goal?

Under what circumstances would you give up? Answering this question in as much detail as possible will be extremely helpful as you work on your goals. Here's an example: If you ask yourself, "What am I ready to do to reach my goals?" and the answer is, "Whatever it takes", you'll need to specify exactly what "whatever it takes" means to you. I encourage you to write your answers down in the "Persevering" section of this book. Coming up with detailed answers to this question will do wonders for your ability to tough things out.

It's more work than you think

Achieving your goals means working harder than you've imagined, and there's nothing wrong with that. That's just how it is. There are many unpredictable factors involved in reaching your goal, and there are some things you can't possibly see coming. Things you thought would be easy may take significantly more time than you expected. Things may change in ways you can't control, and there may be surprises that make your life significantly harder. You might severely underestimate how hard it will be to sell your product, pass a test, or lose weight, which can lead to discouragement.

That's why it's so important to ask yourself the following questions on a regular basis: Am I really doing what it takes to achieve my goal? Could I be doing more? If you have an online business, for instance, you might be spending too much time creating content and not enough on marketing. This happens to a lot of people. In this example, you have to define what "I'll do what it takes to get my name out there" looks like. With that in mind, what more could you do to move closer to your goal?

Day 15

Date: _____

Failing to plan is planning to fail.

— Alan Lakein

Daily goals

-

-

-

-

-

-

Daily tip: *Did you plan to give up as soon as it gets tough?*

When you start to feel like giving up, remember that 95% of the people who feel this way wind up quitting. The first time you feel like giving up is the point where 95% of the people around you quit. The question is, if you always intended to give up when everyone else does, why did you bother setting your goal to begin with? Did you think to yourself, "I'm going to give it a try until it gets tough and then give up like everyone else"? Probably not. So why not take one more step forward and keep pushing through? Strangely enough, we tend to feel like giving up the most right before a breakthrough. I've felt like giving up multiple times when working on my business, so you're by no means alone. Getting the urge to quit is part of the process, but there's no need to give in to it.

Empowering question

What would make you give up on your goal?

Meetings/Appointments	People to contact
Chores	Things to purchase

Distraction crusher

Additional notes (insights, lessons learned etc.)

Day 16

Date: _____

Our emotions need to be as educated as our intellect.

— JIM ROHN

Daily goals:

-

-

-

-

-

-

Daily tips: *Life is a rollercoaster, so enjoy the ride.*

Life is full of ups and downs, and there isn't a successful person on the planet who hasn't experienced this firsthand. You'll have highs and lows as you work on your goals. You may feel great one day only to feel down the next. I experience this at times and it's totally normal. I think the important thing is to avoid becoming overly attached to these transient emotions. They come and go. They always do, because they're nothing if not impermanent. I know, they seem like they'll never go away when they hit you, but they always fade in the end. They'll go away much faster if you refuse to identify with them. When you do this, your negative emotions will no longer be able to trick you, and it will feel almost silly when they try.

Empowering question

Have you ever been so caught up in negative emotions that it seemed they'd never stop? What happened in the end?

Meetings/Appointments	People to contact
Chores	Things to purchase

Distraction crusher

Additional notes (insights, lessons learned etc.)

Day 17

Date: _____

The best years of your life are the ones in which you decide your problems are your own. You do not blame them on your mother, the ecology, or the president. You realize that you control your own destiny.

— ALBERT ELLIS

Daily goals:

-

-

-

-

-

Daily tips: *Pride is your enemy.*

Do you balk at marketing because you think you're above it? Do you refuse to give discounts on your products because of how hard you worked to create them? Do you avoid asking for help because you think you can do everything on your own? If any of these sound familiar, your pride is holding you back. You'll have a hard time achieving your dreams if you allow it to control you. No, your work doesn't deserve to be loved by everybody (especially if you don't promote it). And I'm sorry, but no one cares about how much time and effort it took for any of us to create anything. If you need to give your product a discount, you'll just have to have to suck it up and do it. And no, there's nothing wrong with asking for help. In fact, no one achieves great success all on their own. I encourage you to put your pride aside and do whatever it takes to give your gifts, talents, products, or services to those who need them.

Empowering question

How does pride stand in the way of your goals? Or, if it isn't an issue, how might it pose a problem in the future?

Meetings/Appointments	People to contact
Chores	Things to purchase

Distraction crusher

Additional notes (insights, lessons learned etc.)

Day 18

Date: _____

If you don't like how things are, change it. You're not a tree.

— JIM ROHN

Daily goals:

-

-

-

-

-

-

Daily tips: *Embrace reality to change it.*

Do you have a tendency to deny reality? The more you see reality for what it is, the more you can do to change your current situation. Having the courage to look at our lives with brutal honesty is very powerful, but also pretty challenging. But you can't change something without first admitting that it's there! Aren't where you want to be in life? That's fine, just admit it. You don't have the results you want with your business? Okay, just admit it. There's something you suck at? Just admit it. The key point is to learn to admit things like this without bashing yourself. Try to be as objective as possible. I suck at more things than you can imagine, but it doesn't make me unworthy or incapable of reaching my goals. You are much more than your shortcomings!

Empowering question

Is there an area of your life in which you're deluding yourself?

Meetings/Appointments	People to contact
Chores	Things to purchase

Distraction crusher

Additional notes (insights, lessons learned etc.)

Day 19

Date: _____

Remember, you have been criticizing yourself for years and it hasn't worked. Try approving of yourself and see what happens.

— LOUISE L. HAY

Daily goals

- -
- -
- -
- -
- -
- -

Daily tip

Self-criticism doesn't work.

You may believe that criticizing yourself enables you to persevere, but this is a carrot and stick approach that doesn't work. Research shows that self-compassion is more effective than self-criticism in regards to perseverance. Nobody's perfect. We're all trying our best, so why not show yourself some compassion and take another step towards your goal today? Replace self-criticism with self-compassion for a week and see what happens.

Empowering question

How would your life change if you gave yourself compassion instead of criticism?

Meetings/Appointments	People to contact
Chores	Things to purchase

Distraction crusher

Additional notes (insights, lessons learned etc.)

Day 20

Date: _____

If you can't fly, then run, if you can't run then walk, if you can't walk then crawl, but whatever you do you have to keep moving forward.

— MARTIN LUTHER KING, JR.

Daily goals

-
-
-
-
-
-

Daily tip: *Learn how to motivate yourself when you feel down.*

Are you feeling frustrated, disappointed, or tired? You might not feel any of these things right now, but you're definitely going to feel them at some point. These feelings don't have to sidetrack you, however. They key is to maintain momentum. When you feel down and want to give up, focus on minor tasks and make some tweaks here and there. Anything that's related to your goal will do, even if the relation is vague. It could be something small that only takes a few minutes each day. Just find some way to keep going, however small it may be. This will preserve your momentum while you wait for your motivation to return. It'll come back sooner than you think!

Empowering question

What could you do to motivate yourself when you feel down?

Meetings/Appointments	People to contact
Chores	Things to purchase

Distraction crusher

Additional notes (insights, lessons learned etc.)

Day 21

Date: _____

When I won the Oscar, I thought it was a fluke. I thought everybody would find out, and they'd take it back. They'd come to my house, knocking on the door, 'Excuse me, we meant to give that to someone else. That was going to Meryl Streep.'

— JODIE FOSTER

You think, 'Why would anyone want to see me again in a movie? And I don't know how to act anyway, so why am I doing this?'

— MERYL STREEP

Daily goals

-

-

-

-

-

Daily tips: *It doesn't matter if you feel like a fraud.*

There are already so many people doing what you want to do that you think, "Why bother?" The truth is, you may never stop feeling like a fraud, so why not get used to it? It can lead to getting over it altogether, but there's no need to worry if it continues to linger. Some of the most successful people feel like frauds. There are people who need you and will benefit from what you have to offer. They don't care if you feel like a fraud. Just do what you want to do regardless of these feelings.

Empowering question

Have you ever felt like a fraud? What may be the consequences of using it as an excuse for inaction?

Meetings/Appointments	People to contact
Chores	Things to purchase

Distraction crusher

Additional notes (insights, lessons learned etc.)

STORY OF THE WEEK

Brian Tracy – *Nothing will change until you change*

"Successful people are always looking for opportunities to help others. Unsuccessful people are always asking, 'What's in it for me?'" – Brian Tracy

When those familiar with goal-setting think about the subject, Brian Tracy is probably the first name that comes to mind. Tracy, who has been studying and practicing goal-setting for decades, has taught millions of people across the globe to do the same. He is the author of several best-selling books that discuss goal-setting, time management, and self-discipline.

In one of his videos, Brian Tracy mentioned that there were 3 major turning points in his life. One of them, of course, involved his discovery of goal-setting. Believe it or not, Brian Tracy didn't graduate high-school and lacked formal education for years. At the time of his first turning point, he was sharing a small, one-bedroom apartment with a friend and struggling to make ends meet as a construction worker. After a longstanding routine of waking up at 5 a.m. and taking 3 buses to go to work, he realized that nothing would change until he did. He was struck by the importance of taking responsibility for everything that happened in his life. Does this remind you of anything we talked about before?

His second major turning point came when he discovered goals. In his own words: "I was living on the floor of a friend's one-room apartment. That's all I could find. And I read a little something that said that if you want to be successful you have to have goals and you have to write them down. So I found a scrap of paper - and I can tell you, I was very poor at that time - and I wrote down 10 goals that I would like to achieve."

On this piece of paper, he wrote down goals related to finances and general success, but ultimately lost the piece paper. One month later he realized that he had achieved 8 or 9 of these goals. That's when he realized just how powerful setting written goals could be. Do you know what his third major turning point was? That's right, the discovery of personal development!

Weekly Goal Review – week 3

Congratulations! You've made it to the end of the third week. Facing harsh realities sucks, doesn't it? But you're still with me, and that's what matters.

Now it's time for our weekly review, with the same questions as before.

What went well:

What you could have done better:

Let's look at the progress you made regarding your limiting beliefs and any other obstacles standing in your way.

What went well:

What I could have done better:

If you've discovered any new limiting beliefs, write them down below, along with what you'll do to overcome them. Otherwise, write down your previous limiting beliefs and what you'll do to continue working on them:

My Weekly Goals

My ONE Daily Habit

This is the one habit you'll stick to every day this week (and likely beyond) until you reach your goal.

-

My 3 Core Tasks

These are your most important tasks of the week. They all relate to your 90-Day Goal, and you'll do whatever it takes to achieve them this week.

-

-

-

Other tasks to accomplish (may or may not be related to your goal)

-

-

-

-

-

-

-

LESSON 4

THE POWER OF STICKABILITY — OVERCOMING ANY OBSTACLE THROUGH CONSISTENCY

Do you want to be able to persevere until you achieve your goals? In this lesson, we're going to talk more about consistency. Consistency is crucial for anyone who's serious about achieving their goals, and I'm going to provide a detailed explanation of why this is. Last but not least, we'll talk about ways to become significantly more persistent.

If you want to stay consistent with your goals, it's crucial to build powerful daily habits that support your journey. It's what you do every day that determines whether you'll live the life of your dream or remain perpetually unfulfilled. Trust me when I say that your day-to-day habits have a huge impact on your life. This planner is centered around setting daily goals, so you're already well on your way to creating strong daily habits.

Breaking your goal into daily habits

If you want to work on your goal each day, there's nothing better than breaking it into daily habits. Ask yourself the following question: What's the one thing that, if done every day, would allow me to move closer to my goal? Come up with a list of 10 things you could do, circle the one that would yield the best results, and commit to doing it on a daily basis.

Starting extra small

When you start working on your goals, starting ridiculously small is the best thing you can do to avoid feeling overwhelmed. If you want to get into the habit of meditating, why not start meditating for one minute a day? If you want to exercise every day, why not go for a 3-minute walk first thing every morning? If you want to write a book, why not write 50 words a day? If repeated every day for a long period of time, these seemingly insignificant habits will yield better results than you may think. They'll help you build momentum while creating several positive changes that you cannot yet imagine.

Build and maintain momentum

Momentum is a key component to success. *Here are a few ways you can build momentum:

- **Start ridiculously small.** It'll reduce any friction associated with your habit and will keep you from procrastinating.
- **Resolve to perform your mini-habit every single day, with no exceptions.** This helps you maintain momentum and stay motivated in the long-run.
- **Keep your expectations low: Don't raise your standards for your daily habit.** If your daily habit is going for a 3-minute walk but you wind up doing a 40-minute one, that's awesome. But keep your 3-minute walk habit as it is. That will enable you to stick to your daily habit and build momentum.

*courtesy of Stephen Guise, author of *Mini Habits*

Don't ever give up!

Ever feel like giving up? I've felt like giving up dozens of times while working on my business, and I'm sure I'll feel like giving up plenty of times in the future!

Let me give you one simple yet effective process to increase your perseverance.

1. **Focus on one major goal at a time.** Most people try to do too many things at once. Can you relate to that? If so, stick to one goal until you achieve it. Don't move on to a new task or goal until your current one is complete.
2. **Commit to your goal for a specific amount of time.** For a big goal, giving yourself at least 2 to 3 years is ideal. Make sure you set a clear deadline. A good example would be, "I'll keep working on *insert goal here* until December 31, 2020".
3. **Give yourself permission to give up if AND ONLY IF you reach the deadline.** You can quit if you must once the deadline has passed. Until then, keep working on your goal! I call this deadline the "bullet-proof timeline" for your goal.
4. **If you don't get results, continue to make tweaks and go back to basics.** Go through the course one more time, read the book again, and commit to master whatever you must to achieve your goal. If you do that, you'll see results before you know it.
5. **Remind yourself to be patient.** Each time you feel like giving up, remind yourself that you still have time before your deadline. We often sabotage our chances of success by giving up too early. Learning to be patient has made a major difference in my life, and it worked particularly well when I learned to set a concrete deadline. It gave me a clear timeframe to focus on my goal.

If you combine this process with what we discussed in the previous chapter, you'll develop a high level of persistence. Now for a reminder of the main points of the previous chapter:

- Prepare yourself mentally. Accept that achieving your goal will be much harder than you think, and that this is perfectly okay.
- Visualize your worst-case scenarios so you'll be able to effectively deal with them if they come up in the future.
- Figure out what precisely would make you give up on your goal.

As is the case for most things, consistency is a skill, which means it can be learned. I did, and you can, too!

Day 22

Date: _____

I do not think that there is any other quality so essential to success of any kind as the quality of perseverance. It overcomes almost everything, even nature.

— JOHN D. ROCKEFELLER

Daily goals

-

-

-

-

-

-

Daily tip: *Create a bullet-proof timeline for your goal.*

When you start working on an exciting goal that matters to you, commit to sticking to it for a specific period of time. Make it your main focus during that time period. When another exciting opportunity shows up, say no and refocus. When you feel like giving up, remind yourself that you've committed to that goal for a certain number of months or years. If those months or years have passed without any results, you can consider giving up. Then and only then. Note that I said "consider" giving up. You can always regroup, make changes, and keep going.

Empowering question

Do you have a bullet-proof timeline for your goal? Are you committed to sticking to it?

Meetings/Appointments	People to contact
Chores	Things to purchase

Distraction crusher

Additional notes (insights, lessons learned etc.)

Day 23

Date: _____

To be successful you don't need to do extraordinary things; you just need to do ordinary things extraordinarily well.

— JIM ROHN

Daily goals

-

-

-

-

-

-

Daily tip: *Figuring out whether you'll achieve your goals.*

If you want to know whether you'll succeed, take a look at what you do every day. As we previously discussed, it's what you do every day that determines whether you'll reach your goal. Ask yourself the following question: *If I keep doing what I'm doing today, will I achieve my goals?* If the answer is no, then you might have to make some adjustments. Ask this question every day, and pay close attention to your answers.

Empowering question

Will continuing to do what you did today enable you to achieve your most important goals?

Meetings/Appointments	People to contact
Chores	Things to purchase

Distraction crusher

Additional notes (insights, lessons learned etc.)

Day 24

Date: _____

This quote is distracted by a shiny object. It might be back later...

Daily goals

-

-

-

-

-

-

Daily tip: *Avoid Shiny Object Syndrome!!*

Are you jumping from one course to another, one business idea to the next, or from one opportunity to another, all without success? If this sounds familiar, you may have the Shiny Object Virus. As its name suggests, this virus leads to Shiny Object Syndrome. This syndrome is responsible for many failures, but it's completely avoidable. Once you find something you want to do, commit to it for a good length of time (perhaps 2 to 3 years as mentioned earlier), then stick to it no matter what! That's the bullet-proof timeline we've been talking about. Say no to whatever else pops up, no matter how exciting it may seem. See it for the distraction it is and refocus on your main goal. Stop fooling around and commit to finishing what you're currently working on before moving to another great goal.

Empowering question

Are you suffering from Shiny Object Syndrome? If so, how will you avoid it in the future?

Meetings/Appointments	People to contact
Chores	Things to purchase

Distraction crusher

Additional notes (insights, lessons learned etc.)

Day 25

Date: _____

The best time to plant a tree was 20 years ago. The second best time is now.

— CHINESE PROVERB

Daily goals

-

-

-

-

-

-

Daily tip: *What you do today is what you'll do tomorrow.*

How often do you tell yourself you'll do something tomorrow? How often do you expect your future self to be wiser and more enlightened than your present self? Here's the thing: What you do today is what determines how wise and enlightened your future self will be. Let me ask you a question: If you don't do it today, is it reasonable to expect your future self to do it tomorrow? Always assume that what you do today is what you'll do tomorrow, and evaluate yourself based on that assumption. Your present self creates your future self so take care of future you by doing today what you say you'll do tomorrow.

Empowering question

Think about the person you'll be 5 years from now. What would he or she say to your present self?

Meetings/Appointments	People to contact
Chores	Things to purchase

Distraction crusher

Additional notes (insights, lessons learned etc.)

Day 26

Date: _____

Some things you have to do every day. Eating seven apples on Saturday night instead of one a day just isn't going to get the job done.

— JIM ROHN

Daily goals

-

-

-

-

-

-

Daily tip: *An apple a day keeps the doctor away.*

What if this is true? I'm almost certain it is. After all, your daily habits determine who you'll become in 1 year, 5 years, or even 10 years from now. Your daily habits compound over time and yield results far beyond what you can currently imagine. Just take 5 minutes each day to set goals with this planner and see where you end up in a year. You'll be amazed at the difference a year makes! Alternatively, try asking yourself what you're grateful for each morning and see what happens in the next twelve months. You could also spend the year meditating 5 minutes a day or going for a walk every morning. Of course, bad habits will create major negative changes if continued over the course of a year. Daily habits compound over time, so make sure yours are great ones!

Empowering question

What simple daily habit would have the greatest impact on your life if you stuck to it for the next year? How about the next 5 or 10 years?

Meetings/Appointments	People to contact
Chores	Things to purchase

Distraction crusher

Additional notes (insights, lessons learned etc.)

Day 27

Date: _____

We are what we repeatedly do. Excellence, then, is not an act, but a habit.

— WILL DURANT

Daily goals

-
-
-
-
-
-

Daily tip: *A daily morning ritual can change your life!*

Do you have a routine you follow every morning? I started one back in August of 2016, and it's one of the best choices I ever made. My routine has evolved since I started it, but here's what it currently consists of: 15 minutes of meditation, 10 minutes of stretching, 5 minutes reading and adding entries to my gratitude journal, 5 minutes reading affirmations out loud, a couple minutes reading over my goals, and 5 minutes setting my daily goals. Why not start your own morning ritual? It doesn't have to be long and elaborate, a simple 10 or 15-minute morning ritual can provide a myriad of benefits. (Refer to "My Daily Morning Ritual Checklist" section at the end of this planner)

Empowering question

How could you create an exciting morning ritual that will improve your life?

Meetings/Appointments	People to contact
Chores	Things to purchase

Distraction crusher

Additional notes (insights, lessons learned etc.)

Day 28

Date: _____

> *A man who can't bear to share his habits is a man who needs to quit them.*

— STEPHEN KING

Daily goals

-

-

-

-

-

-

Daily tip: *The compound effect of habits.*

Just spending a few minutes each day on something can yield incredible long-term results. Reading just 10 pages every day would allow you to read about 10 books a year and 100 books in a decade. Writing 500 words a day would allow you to write a book every 3 to 6 months. Listening to audiobooks on your way to work every day would allow you to consume dozens of books each year and hundreds over a decade.

Empowering question

How is setting daily goals improving your life? How could you make the process even more effective?

Meetings/Appointments	People to contact
Chores	Things to purchase

Distraction crusher

Additional notes (insights, lessons learned etc.)

STORY OF THE WEEK

Jim Rohn – *Work harder on yourself than you do on your job*

"'Mr. Rohn, let me see your current list of goals. I've had a lot of experience and I've been out here for a while, so let's go over them and maybe I can really give you some good ideas.' And I said, 'I don't have a list.' He said, 'Well, if you don't have a list of your goals, I can guess your bank balance within a few hundred dollars.' And he did." – Jim Rohn

That's what Jim Rohn's mentor Earl Shoaff said to him when he was 25-years-old and more or less broke. Jim Rohn went on to ask, "You mean to tell me that if I had a list of my goals it would make a difference in my bank account?" to which Earl Shoaff replied, "A drastic difference".

For those of you unfamiliar with him, Jim Rohn was a businessman and one of the most famous personal development figures who mentored the likes of Tony Robbins. He passed away in 2009, but his legacy lives on, and his facebook page is still very active!

At 25, Jim Rohn was an honest worker who didn't mind working overtime. His financial situation wasn't all that great, however, because he was working hard at his job rather than himself. He had a long list of excuses that blamed everything but him for his financial situation.

"It was hard for me to give up my all blame list. It was so comfortable blaming

the government, and blaming my negative relatives, and the company, company policy, union, wage scale, economy, interest rates, prices and circumstances and all that."

With the help of his mentor, Jim Rohn started setting goals and taking responsibility for his life. As a result, he quickly turned his life around and was a millionaire by the age of 30.

Monthly Goal Review ①

Congratulations! You've now made it to the end of the first month. Talk about stickability, baby! That's an important milestone. Take time to celebrate this accomplishment with family or friends if you haven't yet.

We covered four main topics this month, so let's evaluate where you stand on each of them.

- Victim Mentality
- Social Conditioning
- Harsh Reality
- Stickability

I'm going to ask you to rate yourself on a scale of 1 to 10 on each of these topics. This is for you, not me, so be brutally honest with yourself.

Victim Mentality – How much responsibility do you take for your life?

Your score:

Social Conditioning – To what extent are you influenced by social conditioning?

Your score:

Harsh Realities – Have you accepted what it takes to be successful and the harsh reality of how difficult perseverance can be?

Your score:

Stickability – Are you committed to your goal? Are you confident that you'll keep working on it every day until the end of this planner? How about after that?

Your score:

My Weekly Goals

My ONE Daily Habit

This is the one habit you'll stick to every day this week (and likely beyond) until you reach your goal.

-

My 3 Core Tasks

These are your most important tasks of the week. They all relate to your 90-Day Goal, and you'll do whatever it takes to achieve them this week.

-

-

-

Other tasks to accomplish (may or may not be related to your goal)

-

-

-

-

-

-

-

LESSON 5

TURNING YOUR GOAL INTO AN OBSESSION

How often do you think about your goals? Are you obsessed with them? Achieving big goals requires a lot of time and repetition. As mentioned before, working on your goals each day is the only way to build and maintain the momentum required to achieve them.

What's your "why"?

The best way to become obsessed with your goals is to figure out exactly why they matter to you. What makes your current goals so important? Why are they a must for you, and what will happen if you don't achieve them?

Let me give you an example from my life. One of my goals is to create passive income with my books. The way I stated it doesn't convey its significance, yet it's extremely important to me for a variety of reasons. Here are some the benefits of achieving this goal. You'll notice that many of these benefits relate to freedom, which is something I value immensely.

I'll be able to work from anywhere in the world, which will allow me to spend time with my family in France and visit friends who live in different countries.

- I'll be able to travel and learn foreign languages (two things I really enjoy) while working on my business.
- I won't have a boss telling me what to do every day.
- I'll be able to live from my passion, which includes writing, studying, and helping people find their passion.
- I'll be able to free up my time, which will allow me to work on other areas of my life.
- I'll have more time to learn new things, create better books, and help more people.

The value of your goal lies in what it requires you to become.

Another great benefit of my goal is that it requires me to become a better person and develop a high-level mindset. As Jim Rohn says, the real value of a goal is the person you must become to achieve it. This is far more valuable than the goal in itself. Accomplishing my goal means significantly increasing my levels of perseverance, self-esteem, and self-discipline. It requires enhancing my ability to inspire people, improving my marketing strategies, and sharpening my writing skills, among many other things. I must also cut ties with society's standard of conformity and mediocrity that I mentioned in the second lesson.

Your "why" is the most powerful tool you have when it comes to achieving your goals. When you're on the verge of giving up, it's your "why" that will allow you to persevere. It gives you an advantage over others who are pursuing similar goals. When you have a clear "why", you won't be bothered by the things you have to do to reach your goals. Without it, working on your goals would feel like an incessant series of chores.

So, back to you. Why are your goals a must? Use the "My Whys" section to create a list of compelling reasons for pursuing your goals.

Day 29

Date: _____

Ego is the enemy of what you want and of what you have: Of mastering a craft. Of real creative insight. Of working well with others. Of building loyalty and support. Of longevity.

— RYAN HOLIDAY

Daily goals

-

-

-

-

-

Daily tip: *Don't let pride steal your dreams.*

People often fail when pursuing their passion. Naysayers tend to blame these failures on the supposed impracticality or silliness of pursuing your dreams, but that couldn't be further from the truth. The reality is that people fail for a variety of reasons, one of which is pride. A perfect example of this would be artists who refuse to promote themselves. They think everyone should know their work and feel they shouldn't have to do any marketing. That's pretty arrogant, isn't it? When you're first starting out, promote yourself as if your life depends on it. Create free products if you have to. If you're really serious about following your passion, then do whatever it takes! Remember: The world doesn't owe us anything. It's our job to get out there and make things happen.

Empowering question

Are you really doing what it takes to achieve your goals? What else could you be doing?

Meetings/Appointments	People to contact
Chores	Things to purchase

Distraction crusher

Additional notes (insights, lessons learned etc.)

Day 30

Date: _____

Follow your passion, be prepared to work hard and sacrifice, and, above all, don't let anyone limit your dreams.

— DONOVAN BAILEY

Daily goals

-

-

-

-

-

-

Daily tip: *Passion is only half the battle.*

Being passionate will help you persevere and overcome obstacles. But it's a sad fact that many people who start something out of passion give up after a few setbacks. Passion is only part of the equation. The remaining part is your mindset and attitude. Fortunately, using this planner and setting daily goals helps create a powerful mindset that will allow you to achieve your goals. That is, in fact, one of the primary reasons I created this planner.

Empowering question

What's preventing you from doing what you really love?

Meetings/Appointments	People to contact
Chores	Things to purchase

Distraction crusher

Additional notes (insights, lessons learned etc.)

Day 31

Date: _____

Most people spend more time making a list of groceries before they go shopping or planning a vacation than they do in planning their lives.

— BRIAN TRACY

Daily goals

-

-

-

-

-

-

Daily tip: *Read your goals every day.*

By now you should have a list of written goals or tasks, but are you reading it out loud each day? Doing this allows your goals to become part of your reality. When this happens, your subconscious mind kicks in and begins looking for ways to take action towards your goals. It also works to attract the right people and circumstances into your life.

Empowering question

Can you recite your monthly goals from memory?

Meetings/Appointments	People to contact
Chores	Things to purchase

Distraction crusher

Additional notes (insights, lessons learned etc.)

Day 32

Date: _____

> *Everything is always created twice, first in the mind and then in reality.*

— STEPHEN COVEY

Daily goals

-

-

-

-

-

-

Daily tip: *Go beyond daydreaming by repeatedly visualizing your goals.*

Visualize your goals multiple times throughout the day. Where are you? How are you feeling? What are you doing? Here's the trick: don't visualize your goals from a place of hoping they'll happen someday. Instead, visualize them from a place of absolute certainty that they'll happen. When you do this, you take visualization to the next level. You start planting seeds in your mind instead of simply fantasizing. This carries a stronger vibration than daydreaming, which enables your mind to commit to making your visions a reality.

Empowering question

Visualize yourself 10 years from now. Where are you? What kind of person have you become?

Meetings/Appointments	People to contact
Chores	Things to purchase

Distraction crusher

Additional notes (insights, lessons learned etc.)

Day 33

Date: _____

> *One reason so few of us achieve what we truly want is that we never direct our focus; we never concentrate our power. Most people dabble their way through life, never deciding to master anything in particular.*

— TONY ROBBINS

Daily goals

-

-

-

-

-

Daily tip: *When in doubt, go back to basics.*

Many of the world's most successful people continually return to fundamentals. The world's best basketball players practice free throws over and over again. Famous musicians rehearse the same songs day in and day out. Prolific writers edit and rewrite their books repeatedly. I could go on, but the point is that the people in these examples have something in common: They all understand that their ability to master the basics is a critical component to their success.

We often get stuck in a rut because we wrongly assume we've mastered the fundamentals, when we're missing an important piece of the puzzle. If you aren't getting the results you want, go back to basics. Go through the course, book, or video another time or two. Or three. It doesn't matter how many times you have to revisit it as long as you apply everything you learn.

Empowering question

What fundamentals might be missing from your life?

Meetings/Appointments	People to contact
Chores	Things to purchase

Distraction crusher

Additional notes (insights, lessons learned etc.)

Day 34

Date: _____

Obstacles are those frightful things you see when you take your eyes off your goals.

— HENRY FORD

Daily goals

-

-

-

-

-

-

Daily tip: *Think of what you want, not what you don't want.*

Successful people constantly move towards what they want. Unsuccessful people move away from what they don't want. Learn to focus on what you desire instead of worrying about what you don't want. In the same vein, concentrate on where you're going, not where you've been or don't want to be.

Empowering question

How much time do you spend focusing on what you want vs. what you don't want?

Meetings/Appointments	People to contact
Chores	Things to purchase

Distraction crusher

Additional notes (insights, lessons learned etc.)

Day 35

Date: _____

He who has a strong enough why can bear almost any how.

— FRIEDRICH NIETZSCHE

Daily goals

-

-

-

-

-

-

Daily tip: *Find out your "why" and the "how" will take care of itself.*

The stronger your "why" is, the more resourceful you'll be. As I mentioned before, resourcefulness is crucial to achieving any goal. So instead of fixating on the "how", spend time figuring out your "why". As Jim Rohn said, "When the 'why' gets stronger, the 'how' gets easier". A strong "why" provides excellent fuel and compels you to take action. When you continually take action, the "how" will start to unfold.

Empowering question

How could you strengthen the "why" behind your current goals?

Meetings/Appointments	People to contact
Chores	Things to purchase

Distraction crusher

Additional notes (insights, lessons learned etc.)

STORY OF THE WEEK

The stories of Mrs. D – *Use goals to improve your health*

Goals can be very powerful, especially in extreme cases. To that end, here's an inspiring story from *The Magic of Thinking Big*, a class book by David J. Schwartz.

"Goals, intense goals, can keep a person alive when nothing else will. Mrs. D., the mother of a college friend of mine, contracted cancer when her son was only two. To darken matters, her husband had died only three months before her illness was diagnosed. Her physicians offered little hope. But Mrs. D. would not give up. She was determined that she would see her two-year-old son through college by operating a small retail store left to her by her husband. There were numerous surgical operations. Each time the doctors would say, "Just a few more months." The cancer was never cured. But those "few more months" stretched into 20 years. She saw her son graduated from college. Six weeks later she was gone."

If you were previously unsure of whether you should have goals in your life, this is probably pretty convincing. If a burning desire can keep someone with cancer alive for 20 years, imagine what your burning desire can do for you in the coming years!

Weekly Goal Review – week 5

Congratulations! You've made it to the end of the fifth week. Your obsession knows no limit!

Let's go over the week together.

What went well:

What you could have done better:

Let's look at the progress you made regarding your limiting beliefs and any other obstacles that stand in your way.

What went well:

What I could have done better:

If you've discovered any new limiting beliefs, write them down below, along with what you'll do to overcome them. Otherwise, write down your previous limiting beliefs and what you'll do to continue working on them:

My Weekly Goals

My ONE Daily Habit

This is the one habit you'll stick to every day this week (and likely beyond) until you reach your goal.

-

My 3 Core Tasks

These are your most important tasks of the week. They all relate to your 90-Day Goal, and you'll do whatever it takes to achieve them this week.

-

-

-

Other tasks to accomplish (may or may not be related to your goal)

-

-

-

-

-

-

-

LESSON 6

FAILURE AS A TEACHER: BECOMING UNSTOPPABLE BY
REFRAMING FAILURE

Are you afraid of failure? Do you see it as a negative experience? Unfortunately, society as a whole has a very unhealthy relationship with failure. Redefining the meaning you give to failure is the only way to avoiding becoming a "failure". By this I mean that you'll never be able to reach your full potential. To be honest, you won't even reach a fraction of it. You'll never know what you're truly capable of, and this is one of the very few ways in which you can genuinely fail.

Success and failure are two sides of the same coin

You can't have success without failure. They work together and are intrinsically linked. If you think you can accomplish your goals without failing, you're only deluding yourself.

Failure is just a sign that it's time to make adjustments

Failure might seem like a horrible, daunting thing, but it exists to guide and warn you when you go off track. It tells you that you need to make some modifications. How else would you know that you need to change something? If you think about it, failure, at least as we know it, is nonexistent. It's a shame that the vast majority of us were taught to avoid it at all costs.

Can you imagine what life would be like without fear of failure? You'd be able to bounce back from setbacks and keep trying until you get the results you want. How amazing would that be? Wouldn't you have a significantly better chance of achieving your goals? There's a better, more empowering word you can use instead of failure: feedback. When it comes to defining failure appropriately, the word feedback is as constructive as it is accurate. Viewing your setbacks as feedback presupposes that you're going to learn something from failure. That assumption is quite powerful. The more feedback you get, the more you can adjust your path until you reach your final destination.

Failure is normal

Success is never a linear path. There will be ups and downs, and you'll encounter multiple setbacks along the way. You'll face disappointment, frustration, and jealousy. You'll also wrestle with fear, doubt, and insecurity. This is perfectly normal. Avoid the trap of thinking you failed because you aren't good enough, smart enough, or talented enough. Nothing's wrong with you aside from thinking that you can experience success without failure. No one can do that, so stop holding yourself to an impossible standard.

Real failure isn't failing to get results

Genuine failure is not trying. Genuine failure is when you know what you're supposed to do but never bother to do it. That's what real failure looks like.

We've been conditioned to believe that results are all that matter. But that's pretty impractical considering the fact that we can't necessarily control results. We can, on the other hand, control our actions, which is why what we do is far more important than the results we get.

The question isn't whether or not you got results, it's whether you took the right action. If not, did you learn from it? Did you take that course, write that book, or stick to your new habit? If you did what you said you'd do, the outcome is immaterial. It's really important to focus on taking the right actions and the process in general. In doing so, you'll be able to minimize your fear of failure. When you stop worrying about the outcome, failure stops being such a big deal.

If you continually take the right actions and learn as much as you can from the experiences that follow, you'll eventually get the results you want.

Day 36

Date: _____

The fastest way to succeed is to double your failure rate.

— Thomas J. Watson

Daily goals

-

-

-

-

-

-

Daily tip: *You are going to fail.*

Again, failure is as unavoidable as it is normal. You're going to experience failure several times throughout your journey, and that's exactly how it should be. Failure isn't a problem, but your relationship with it might be. When you have the courage and humility to learn from every "failure" you experience, great things happen. These learning opportunities will ultimately put you ahead of the pack. If you can step back and see your failures for what they truly are, you'll become unstoppable.

Empowering question

What would you do if you had no fear of failure?

Meetings/Appointments	People to contact
Chores	Things to purchase

Distraction crusher

Additional notes (insights, lessons learned etc.)

Day 37

Date: _____

For every failure, there's an alternative course of action. You just have to find it. When you come to a roadblock, take a detour.

— MARY KAY ASH, FOUNDER OF MARY KAY COSMETICS.

Daily goals

-

-

-

-

-

-

Daily tip: *There are billions of choices you can make at any given time.*

We all operate with certain beliefs and have patterns that guide our decisions. These patterns can severely undermine our ability to think outside the box. When this happens, it's difficult to come up with solutions to our obstacles. Keep asking yourself whether you could do things differently. Is there anybody who could help you? Is there a way you could achieve your goals 10 times faster? What bold action could you take? What crazy ideas can you come up with?

Empowering question

Can you come up with a new idea that will enhance your ability to achieve your goal?

Meetings/Appointments	People to contact
Chores	Things to purchase

Distraction crusher

Additional notes (insights, lessons learned etc.)

Day 38

Date: _____

When the going gets tough, put one foot in front of the other and just keep going. Don't give up.

— ROY T. BENNETT

Daily goals

-

-

-

-

-

-

Daily tip: *You'll succeed because most people give up on their goals.*

The vast majority of people with goals will give up in the end. But will you? If you stick with your goal and take consistent action each day, you're bound to find success. Remember the bullet-proof timeline I mentioned earlier? Keep going until you reach that bullet-proof timeline and don't even think about quitting until the deadline has arrived. When things don't work out, make some adjustments and take more action. Although few people want to hear it, hard work and consistent action can solve the vast majority of problems.

Empowering question

Did you plan your goal with the intention of giving up midstream?

Meetings/Appointments	People to contact
Chores	Things to purchase

Distraction crusher

Additional notes (insights, lessons learned etc.)

Day 39

Date: _____

Never, never, never give up.

Daily goals

-

-

-

-

-

-

Daily tip: *You'll feel like giving up so get used to it*

The urge to give up will come many, many times, so you might as well get used to it.

Like most people, I've felt like giving up more times than I can count, and I know the feeling will crop up countless times in the future. I had periods of intense self-doubt. I kept questioning what I was doing with my life and wondering if it all made sense. Everyone goes through this, so it's crucial to be prepared for it. Pressing on when you want to give up strengthens your perseverance, which will eventually make it easier to keep going.

Empowering question

Do you know what you'll do when you feel like giving up?

Meetings/Appointments	People to contact
Chores	Things to purchase

Distraction crusher

Additional notes (insights, lessons learned etc.)

Day 40

Date: _____

I can accept failure; everyone fails at something. But I can't accept not trying.

— Michael Jordan

Daily goals

-

-

-

-

-

-

Daily tip: *If you don't try, you've already failed.*

Okay, so you're afraid of failure. But what if I told you that you've failed thousands of times in the past without knowing it? That's right, you failed every time fear kept you from trying. By refusing to give it a shot, you gave up on yourself and turned your back on your potential. You ignored your ability to use failure as a means to grow into a better you. You downplayed your greatness time and time again. How much longer can you keep doing that?

Empowering question

Can you think of a time when not trying stopped you from getting the results you wanted?

Meetings/Appointments	People to contact
Chores	Things to purchase

Distraction crusher

Additional notes (insights, lessons learned etc.)

Day 41

Date: _____

There is no such thing as failure, only learning.

— TONY ROBBINS

Daily goals

-

-

-

-

-

-

Daily tips: *Substitutes for an ugly word.*

I don't like the word failure, so I'm going to give you alternative words that will help you change your perception of failure. Failure can be labeled as any of the following:

- A learning opportunity
- A source of valuable insights
- A temporary setback
- A brief pit stop
- Constructive feedback
- A wake-up call

There are plenty of other empowering words you can use to replace failure. Brainstorm for a bit and see what you come up with.

Empowering question

Think of your most recent failure. How do the substitute words apply to your situation?

Meetings/Appointments	People to contact
Chores	Things to purchase

Distraction crusher

Additional notes (insights, lessons learned etc.)

Day 42

Date: _____

I have not failed. I've just found 10,000 ways that won't work.

— THOMAS EDISON

Daily goals

-
-
-
-
-
-

Daily tip: *Your brain learns by failing*

Your brain is designed to solve problems and achieve goals. However, if you don't provide it with enough feedback, including the so-called failures, it won't be able to do its job and you won't achieve your goals. Make sure you give your brain enough feedback by constantly trying out new things and learning from them. People who end up succeeding always failed way more often than other people.

Empowering question

Think of the biggest failure in your life. What did you learn from it and how did it change your life in a positive way?

Meetings/Appointments	People to contact
Chores	Things to purchase

Distraction crusher

Additional notes (insights, lessons learned etc.)

STORY OF THE WEEK

Arnold Schwarzenegger– *Whatever it takes to get there I would do*

"Everyone was saying this is the wrong direction that I'm going, or I'm in a dream world, I'm useless. Whatever it was, I said, I'm gonna break through that. No matter what it takes, I needed to reach that goal, that vision that I had of being a world champion." – Arnold Schwarzenegger

When it comes to turning a vision or goal into reality, very few can match Arnold Schwarzenegger's impressive track record. Schwarzenegger was born in a small village in Austria where bodybuilding was completely nonexistent. Despite this, he managed to stumble upon a magazine featuring 3-time Mr. Universe winner Reg Park. As Schwarzenegger himself likes to say, this magazine laid out the whole blueprint regarding what he wanted to do.

Upon reading the magazine, he decided to become Mr. Universe. He began visualizing himself with the perfect body. He looked at pictures of bodybuilders every morning to remind himself of his vision and what he wanted his body to look like. This huge, compelling vision was an extremely powerful motivator that left him pumped each time he went to the gym and excited to make things happen.

While others burnt out, he was genuinely content and excited to work out 4 or 5 hours a day. His enthusiasm came from the knowledge that every single rep was moving him closer to his dream. He used the same blueprint mentioned above to become a movie star, and again to become the Governor of California.

Arnold Schwarzenegger teaches us that, before anything else, we must first have a clear and compelling vision of what we want to accomplish. This vision has to be something that genuinely motivates us to take action towards becoming the person we envision.

To achieve extraordinary results, we also have to focus on one huge goal at a time. This allows us to build the perfect momentum and create much-needed energy through laser-sharp focus.

Weekly Goal Review – week 6

Congratulations! You've made it to the end of the sixth week. You're almost halfway through. You're probably one of those people who can keep going no matter how many setbacks arise. I like that!

Now it's time for our weekly review.

What went well:

What you could have done better:

Let's look at the progress you made regarding your limiting beliefs and any other obstacles that stand in your way.

What went well:

What I could have done better:

If you've discovered any new limiting beliefs, write them down below, along with what you'll do to overcome them. Otherwise, write down your previous limiting beliefs and what you'll do to continue working on them:

My Weekly Goals

My ONE Daily Habit

This is the one habit you'll stick to every day this week (and likely beyond) until you reach your goal.

-

My 3 Core Tasks

These are your most important tasks of the week. They all relate to your 90-Day Goal, and you'll do whatever it takes to achieve them this week.

-

-

-

Other tasks to accomplish (may or may not be related to your goal)

-

-

-

-

-

-

-

LESSON 7

BEATING PROCRASTINATION AND SUPERCHARGING YOUR PRODUCTIVITY

We've talked about the dangers of procrastination briefly in the introduction but it's damaging enough to warrant revisiting. If you want to beat it once and for all, you need to think about the benefits of avoiding it. What would happen if you stopped procrastinating altogether? Can you imagine how much more you'd get done? In this lesson, we're going to delve deeper into procrastination and learn how to destroy it.

No matter how exciting your goals are, there will be times when you'll feel like procrastinating. This urge might come from fatigue or fear, to name just a few potential causes. Whatever the case, your ability to be productive has more to do with how well you understand your mind than with the productivity tips or strategies you use. Not even the best method in the world could take the place of knowing the inner workings of your mind. The mind is a powerful thing. You've got two choices: Control it, or let it control you. For optimal productivity, you'll need to choose the first option.

I'm going to let you in on 3 secrets that will help you master your mind and leave procrastination in the dust. Once you get the hang of these 3 procrastination-busters, your mind will have a hard time convincing you to put things off. This will allow you to get better results as you work toward your goals.

But before we get started, let's take a closer look at procrastination.

Why Do We Procrastinate?

Picture this: You're motivated and beyond ready to work on your primary task. You're raring to go---until you feel a sudden, powerful urge to grab a coffee, check Facebook, call a friend, or go for a walk. You just want to do something else. Anything else. You want to escape in any way you can.

Sound familiar? If so, have you ever tried to figure out what you're running from? You're probably trying to escape fear. Fear that you won't do a good job, fear that you aren't good enough, or fear that you can't complete the task. The key here is learning to feel your fear and take action in spite of it. And now for the 3 secrets that will enable you to do just that.

1. Eliminate Distractions

Start by minimizing the potential for distractions since virtually any distraction can become tempting when the urge to procrastinate strikes. Here's what you can do to get rid of them:

Use a time log to find any "procrastination patterns". Record everything you do throughout the day. Where are you wasting time? Why? How much is due to procrastination?

Create a Not-To-Do List based on the time log results. Put the list on your desk so you can see it easily. (ex: Don't check emails, don't go on YouTube etc.)

- Don't check emails.
- Don't check Facebook or social media.
- Don't go on YouTube or Google.
- Don't go for a walk.
- Don't check my phone.
- Don't eat.

- Don't check my Amazon book sales.
- Don't go to the convenience store to buy a drink.

The next line of defense is removing all distractions from your desk. You should also plan your tasks in advance, prepare your environment, and give yourself a way to jot down intrusive thoughts. These include remembering things you need to do, light bulb moments, and new ideas. Doing this will keep you from spending an hour on Facebook when all you really wanted to do was send a quick email to a friend. I included the "Distraction crusher" section for this very reason. I highly encourage you to take full advantage of them!

Make sure you keep phones, books, food, and other distracting items far away. I always clear my desk before I start working. It makes focusing so much easier. This felt strange when I first began doing it, but the more I did it, the more habitual it became. It's now ingrained to the point that it serves as a signal to my brain. When I clear my desk, my mind understands that it's "work time".

The day before you start working on your task, you can also spend some time visualizing yourself doing it. This will help you condition your mind and decrease the risk of distractions.

You can prepare your environment by readying the tools you'll need for your task ahead of time. Make sure everything is easily accessible. Do any and everything you can to make things as effortless as possible.

2. Become Aware of Your Fears and Emotions

It's essential to get in touch with the feelings that come up when you're about to start working on an important task. What is that feeling that makes you want to procrastinate and escape? Stay with that feeling. Face it. Look at it closely. It's nothing more than your mind trying to trick you. See how that works? Becoming aware of your feelings will reduce the likelihood you procrastinate.

Simply becoming aware of your feelings and understanding how they work will provide a significant increase in your self-control. Is your mind tired, bored, or scared? Well, guess what? It doesn't matter! You are NOT your mind, so train yourself to act in spite of it.

3. Reduce the Friction Associated with Starting the Task

It's crucial to reduce the discomfort involved in beginning your task. You can accomplish this through visualization. Consider your current feelings and imagine how you'll feel once your task is completed. If that doesn't work, just start and see what happens. Tell yourself you'll only work on it for five minutes. You can do almost anything for five minutes, right?

If worse comes to worst, accept the possibility that you may not do as good of a job as you'd like. Make it okay to do poorly. Unless you're extremely tired, you'll probably do just fine.

But what if you *genuinely* think you'll do a subpar job? Well, assuming that's really true, what makes you think you'll do any better tomorrow or next week? After all, your plan was to start *today*, not tomorrow, the day after tomorrow, or any other day.

If you've read this far, I'm afraid you've run out of excuses to procrastinate.

These productivity tips are just the beginning when it comes to improving the way you work on your goals. Let's look at a few ways you can make yourself even more effective.

Work in Blocks to Maximize Efficiency

Working in blocks is a great way to stay on task and maintain your productivity. All you have to do is adjust to working on things for specific chunks of time. For optimal results, try 90-Minute Blocks, the Pomodoro Technique, or the 52/17 Method. If you're not familiar with any of these, that's okay, keep reading for a detailed description of each system.

A. 90-Minute Blocks

Implementing this method involves devoting 90 minutes to your most important tasks. Treat those 90 minutes as sacred: No interruptions allowed. Don't eat, don't drink. Don't go to the bathroom (unless you *really* need to). Don't check your emails, look at your phone, or watch TV. Focus! It's helpful to declutter your space before the 90-minute block as well. Clutter breeds distractions, and a clean space makes it easier to concentrate.

After the 90 minutes are up, take a 15, 20, or 30-minute break to clear your mind. It's best to completely disconnect from whatever you were working on. Spend your break doing something that refreshes you. This could mean going for a walk, reading a book, meditating, or taking a nap. It all depends on what relaxes you.

B. The 52/17 Method

Although it may seem random, recent studies have shown that the most productive employees are those who take a 17-minute break for every 52 minutes of work. The reason for this is not yet fully understood, but that doesn't mean you can't use this mysterious ratio to increase your own productivity.

C. The Pomodoro Technique

This method entails working on tasks in 20-minute sessions, all of which are punctuated by a 5-minute break. After four 20-minute sessions you can stretch your breaks to 15, 20, or 30 minutes.

Choosing the Right Block Method

By now you might be wondering which technique is best. Well, that all depends. Everyone is different, so it's up to you to try them out and tweak the timeframes until you find what suits you. I prefer spending at least one hour on a task before I take a break, and 90 minutes is my sweet spot.

That said, some techniques are better than others when it comes to specific tasks. With that in mind, consider the following recommendations:

- For tasks that require a lot of concentration, try 90-Minute Blocks. If, for instance, you want to write an article, it's best to spend at least 90 minutes working on it before you take a break. Shorter amounts of time have the potential to disrupt your flow, which increases the amount of time it takes to finish your task.

- If the task at hand will take roughly an hour complete, the 52/17 Method is your best bet.
- For tasks that don't require much concentration or creativity, the Pomodoro Technique is optimal. According to Robin Sharma, it takes 21 minutes to refocus after you've been distracted. As such, the Pomodoro Technique is best used for repetitive tasks that aren't mentally taxing.

Remember, you don't need to follow these techniques to the letter. The point is getting yourself to fully focus on a task without any distractions. You need to avoid multitasking at all costs, so do whatever boosts your concentration the most.

Day 43

Date: _____

The hardest part of any important task is getting started on it in the first place. Once you actually begin work on a valuable task, you seem to be naturally motivated to continue.

— BRIAN TRACY

Daily goals

-

-

-

-

-

-

Daily tip: *Just get started.*

It's always hard to force yourself to work on an important task when you'd rather be doing something else. Once you get started, however, it's amazing how quickly you can get absorbed in the task. You might even get on a roll. When you find that you're really struggling to start a task, set aside a few minutes to devote to it. Give yourself permission to stop when time is up, then start working. This will often be the push you need to go full speed ahead with your task. Don't be surprised if you look up and find you've been at it for hours!

Empowering question

What are the consequences of procrastination in your life? Make a list of the problems it's creating.

Meetings/Appointments	People to contact
Chores	Things to purchase

Distraction crusher

Additional notes (insights, lessons learned etc.)

Day 44

Date: _____

Much of the stress that people feel doesn't come from having too much to do. It comes from not finishing what they started.

— David Allen

Daily goals

-

-

-

-

-

-

Daily tip: *Do it first thing in the morning.*

Start working on your most important task or goal first thing in the morning, and stick with it until it's done. This is a very effective way to build momentum. You'll get a confidence boost when you complete the task, and this will infuse the rest of your day with positive energy. More importantly, this tactic makes it harder to make excuses. If you start something as soon as you wake up, there isn't much time to come up with ways to put it off.

Empowering question

What one thing could you do first thing in the morning that would have the greatest impact on your day?

Meetings/Appointments	People to contact
Chores	Things to purchase

Distraction crusher

Additional notes (insights, lessons learned etc.)

Day 45

Date: _____

Everyone procrastinates. The difference between high performers and low performers is largely determined by what they choose to procrastinate on.

— BRIAN TRACY

Daily goals

-

-

-

-

-

-

Daily tip: *Procrastinate on the right thing.*

We all procrastinate to some extent, but what are your own personal ways of doing it? Are you binge-watching videos on YouTube while pretending it's somehow related to your goals? Are you spending your time on low-impact activities that you pass off as work? If this sounds familiar, you're not alone. You may not be able to fully eliminate procrastination, but you can find a more strategic way of doing it. You could, for instance, make a list of small tasks that will move you closer to your goals but require little effort. When you don't feel like working on the task at hand, spending a few minutes on something easy yet relevant can help you build momentum until you're ready to tackle something bigger. Worst case scenario, you'll preserve your momentum while getting a few things done.

Empowering question

What tasks could you choose to procrastinate with to maintain momentum?

Meetings/Appointments	People to contact
Chores	Things to purchase

Distraction crusher

Additional notes (insights, lessons learned etc.)

Day 46

Date: _____

Do you know what happens when you give a procrastinator a good idea? Nothing!

— Donald Gardner

Daily goals

-

-

-

-

-

-

Daily tip: *Using visualization to avoid procrastination.*

When you set your daily goals, take a few seconds to visualize yourself starting and completing each task on your list. Then make a commitment to them! When it's time get to work, you'll be less apt to procrastinate.

Empowering question

Visualize yourself completing your tasks for the day. How would you feel after they're all done?

Meetings/Appointments	People to contact
Chores	Things to purchase

Distraction crusher

Additional notes (insights, lessons learned etc.)

Day 47

Date: _____

Just enough sense to stick with something – a chore, task, project – until it's completed, pays off much better than idle intelligence, even if idle intelligence be of genius caliber. For stickability is 95 percent of ability.

— David J. Schwartz

Daily goals

-

-

-

-

-

-

Daily tip: *Finish everything you start.*

Whenever you have to go back to something that isn't fully completed, you lose momentum and energy. Whenever possible, train yourself to finish your current task before moving to another. Start practicing with small tasks like sending emails. Learning to stay with a task until it's 100% done will enhance your self-discipline and increase your self-esteem. It also frees your mind to focus on other things without unfinished tasks looming in the background. Last but not least, sticking to things until they're done will cure any issues with perfectionism that you may have by taking away opportunities to nitpick.

Empowering question

What tasks do you tend to leave unfinished?

Meetings/Appointments	People to contact
Chores	Things to purchase

Distraction crusher

Additional notes (insights, lessons learned etc.)

Day 48

Date: _____

You cannot eat every tadpole and frog in the pond, but you can eat the biggest and ugliest one, and that will be enough, at least for the time being.

— Brian Tracy

Daily goals

-

-

-

-

-

-

Daily tip: *Procrastination in disguise.*

Procrastination can manifest in many different ways. Ultimately, any activity or behavior can become procrastination when used as a way to put things off. Have you ever felt the sudden urge to watch a video, check your mail, call a friend, or go for a walk just as you're about to start an important task? If so, that's your mind trying to find an escape from what it knows you should be doing. Are you aware of the ways in which you procrastinate? Being aware of your behavior is the first step toward overcoming chronic procrastination.

Empowering question

What makes you procrastinate and how exactly do you do it?

Meetings/Appointments	People to contact
Chores	Things to purchase

Distraction crusher

Additional notes (insights, lessons learned etc.)

Day 49

Date: _____

A wise man will be a master of his mind, a fool will be its slave.

— PUBLILIUS SYRUS

Daily goals

-

-

-

-

-

-

Daily tip: *You are* not *your mind.*

You don't always have to listen to your mind, let alone obey it. Feeling tired after work doesn't mean you should put things off and skip working on your goal for the day. You're bigger than your mind, and there's a part of you that can do much more than what your mind says you can. NAVY seals use something called the 40 % rule to cope with exhaustion. They tell themselves that fatigue is their mind trying to stop them, which means they can actually keep going. You can apply this same rule to yourself. You can either be the master of your mind or a slave to it, the choice is solely yours.

Empowering question

How does your mind dictate what you should and shouldn't do?

Meetings/Appointments	People to contact
Chores	Things to purchase

Distraction crusher

Additional notes (insights, lessons learned etc.)

STORY OF THE WEEK

Grant Cardone – *It's not just wants, it's goals*

"Either clarify what you want, or somebody else's gonna clarify what they want and you're gonna spend your lifetime working for them." – Grant Cardone

Grant Cardone didn't have a particularly easy childhood. His father died of a heart attack when he was just 10-years-old, and growing up without his guidance was difficult. In high school, he had issues with authority that led to drug and alcohol abuse. His substance abuse problem prevented him from keeping a job. He was described as of "out of control" and "troubled" during his teenage years and early adulthood. This state of affairs left him bitter and resentful.

At twenty, he lost his older brother, which was yet another hit to his family, sense of direction, and life in general.

Later, in his early twenties, he was beaten within inches of his life. He bears the scars to this day.

His drug problem progressed to the point where he had to put himself in a treatment facility. At 25, he was broke, emotionally exhausted, and a problem for both society and his family.

Today, at age 58, he's close to becoming a billionaire. Emotionally, he's never been happier. He wakes up each day with purpose. In Cardone's own words, he knows where he's going and what he's doing. If you knew him 35 years ago and compared him with who he is today, you might believe in miracles.

Cardone is also a big believer in setting goals. He writes his goals down every day, sometimes even twice daily (at the beginning and end of each day).

In addition to setting daily goals, he sets new exciting goals 1 to 3 times a year. He takes his wife and children on a ship and they answer questions together that clarify the following 3 things:

1. Where they're going
2. Why they're going there (or, in other words, the purpose of their journey and what keeps them excited about it)
3. What they really want

The last point is important enough to be repeated. Cardone himself says, "I don't think in terms of goals as much as I think in terms of what I want".

He and his family go through this exercise over the course of several days. Read on for a quick look at what it entails.

First day – Writing down what he wants

On day 1, he simply writes down what he'd like to see happen. At this point, he doesn't think about how he's going to do it. He just focuses on what he wants and what he'd ideally like to achieve within the year.

Subsequent days – Clarifying goals and setting priorities

In the days that follow, Cardone spends his time clarifying these goals by writing them down over and over again. With each repetition, he gets a better understanding of which goals he's truly excited and passionate about. He still doesn't think about how he'll accomplish them.

He goes through this process with both his family and the executives in his company.

In summary, Grant Cardone's process is as follows:

- Figure out what you want and what drives you

- Don't worry about how you're going to do it

- Clarify what you want over a period of several days

Weekly Goal Review – week 7

Congratulations! You've made it to the end of the seventh week. Continue with the process and keep up the good work to reach your 90-Day goal.

Let's see how much progress you've made on your ONE goal.

What went well:

What you could have done better:

Let's look at the progress you made regarding your limiting beliefs and any other obstacles that stand in your way.

What went well:

What I could have done better:

If you've discovered any new limiting beliefs, write them down below, along with what you'll do to overcome them. Otherwise, write down your previous limiting beliefs and what you'll do to continue working on them:

My Weekly Goals

My ONE Daily Habit

This is the one habit you'll stick to every day this week (and likely beyond) until you reach your goal.

-

My 3 Core Tasks

These are your most important tasks of the week. They all relate to your 90-Day Goal, and you'll do whatever it takes to achieve them this week.

-

-

-

Other tasks to accomplish (may or may not be related to your goal)

-

-

-

-

-

-

-

LESSON 8

COMMITTING TO MASTERY

Are you truly committed to mastering the skills you need? This lesson will touch upon some important concepts that must be grasped if you want to reach your goals. These concepts, which work for both current and future goals, will provide a lifetime of benefits.

Overcoming Shiny Object Syndrome

We talked a little about this issue earlier, but it's important enough to touch on again. Jumping from thing to thing prevents you from achieving even a fraction of the success you could have if you'd just stick to something. I can't stress this enough. <u>Your ability to stick to your goal is one of the most important factors in getting results.</u> When you have a goal, fully commit to it. Stick to it until you get the results you want, even if that takes more time and effort than expected.

Thinking "I already know that"

Never assume that you've tried everything or there's little left to learn. It's almost impossible to know something extremely well without being able to get results with it. You need to be honest with yourself and ask these questions: Do I really, really know it? Am I doing it and living it, or is it just something I somewhat know intellectually? Let's take goal-setting as an example. You'd need to ask yourself if you're embodying it by setting goals every day and getting concrete results from the process? Have you mastered it, or could you be missing some key things? If you can't put something into practice in a way that yields results, you have a lot more to learn.

You don't want to be the guy who tells everyone they should be doing a certain thing when he's not doing it himself. If you're brutally honest with yourself, you'll realize that you don't know as much as you thought you did. You might know something on a superficial level, but you'll need to gain a deeper understanding if you want tangible results. Beware of the "I already know that" mindset and stay humble enough to go back to basics when you fail to get the results you want.

Focusing on the process

Accomplishing something big is never easy. You'll want to give up countless times and you're going to feel like your hard work isn't paying off. That's why it's crucial to focus on the process rather than results. You can't predict if your next book will be a best-seller, but you have total control of your ability to stick to writing it.

Learn to enjoy the process and congratulate yourself for taking the right actions. That should be your real motivation and source of pride. Forget about the results for a while and ask yourself, "Did I take the right action today?"

Repetition is your friend

How often do you reread a book, re-watch a video, or go through a course one more time? Repetition is a key part of success. Even the world's best athletes are constantly working on fundamental moves. If your fundamentals are weak, your growth will be very limited. You'll get better results reading a self-help book 10 times than reading 10 different self-help books. Knowledge is power, but only when it's fully absorbed and leads to action. When you fall short on results, always go over what you've learned in the past. See if there's something you missed. You might need to do something more, less, or differently. Or perhaps you need to be more consistent. Whatever the case may be, you won't learn much without a certain level of repetition. Personally, I like to focus on one or two books and read them until I'm able to use what I've learned. I continually revisit them to see if there's more to learn.

Always think long-term

It's easy to fall into short-term thinking and forget the big picture. We're inundated with literal and figurative "magic pills". These quick fixes claim to solve our problems with little to no effort. This makes it harder to remember that success requires time and effort. When you experience short-term setbacks, your long-term vision will motivate you to stay consistent. That's why it's so important to focus on your vision as much as possible. Try to keep it in the back of your mind every day. Focus on the big picture, maintain consistency, and, most importantly, enjoy the process.

Never, ever give up.

Most people give up way too soon. You won't always get the results you expected. It's a cycle that has its ups and downs. You're going to feel stuck, frustrated, tired, and depressed. I can't remember how many times I got into funks and doubted myself. "What am I doing with my life?" and "Why am I writing books nobody reads anyway?" were among the thoughts I struggled with. I'd be lying if I said I'm never tempted to give up, but continuing to push forward despite my feelings has made me more persistent. It'll do the same for you, too. Things won't necessarily get easier, but you'll get stronger, which will make things *feel* easier.

Focus on continuous improvement

In an ever-changing world, you have to be able to learn, work on yourself, and improve your craft on a regular basis. This is one of the most valuable skills you can develop. You can always learn more, and there's always room for improvement. Productivity, communication skills, writing, perseverance, you name it. You can learn anything and there's always some way to get better. Even if you get a late start, it's possible to master virtually anything that's important enough to you.

Day 50

Date: _____

Success is a process, a quality of mind and way of being, an outgoing affirmation of life.

— ALEX NOBLE

Daily goals

-

-

-

-

-

-

Daily tip: *Focus on the process.*

I've said it before and I'll say it again: You have to focus on the process. It's depressing when things don't move as quickly as they should. It might seem like everyone else is extremely far ahead of you, and you may even feel completely hopeless. It doesn't take much to get trapped in waves of negativity. When you do, always remember to refocus on the process. Set your goals and get the necessary tasks done to the best of your ability each day. Do that and you'll inevitably reach your goals. What else is there to do, anyway?

Empowering question:

What could you do to ensure you focus on the process instead of the results?

Meetings/Appointments	People to contact
Chores	Things to purchase

Distraction crusher

Additional notes (insights, lessons learned etc.)

Day 51

Date: _____

Faith is taking the first step even when you don't see the whole staircase.

— MARTIN LUTHER KING, JR

Daily goals

-
-
-
-
-
-

Daily tip: *Believe in the inevitability of your success.*

Things may not work out the way you expected, but have faith that you'll eventually get results. Your faith and ability to believe in yourself are some of your most important assets. With them, anything is possible. Without them, nothing is possible. You really have to think about your goal every day and obsess about it. This is one of the few areas in life where obsession is beneficial. Obsessing over your goals helps you push through rough patches and strengthen your belief that it's really going to happen.

Empowering question:

How could you strengthen your faith and believe in yourself more?

Meetings/Appointments	People to contact
Chores	Things to purchase

Distraction crusher

Additional notes (insights, lessons learned etc.)

Day 52

Date: _____

> *I fear not the man who has practiced 10,000 kicks once, but I fear the man who had practiced one kick 10,000 times.*

— B<small>RUCE</small> L<small>EE</small>

Daily goals

-

-

-

-

-

-

Daily tip: *Repetition is better than novelty.*

We all enjoy new things. We like going to new places, seeing new movies, reading new books, and hearing new music. But the fact remains that you'll never get what you want if you continually bounce around from one thing to the next. As exciting as the new is, you must learn to appreciate and enjoy repetition. You have to fall in love with the process of digging deeper into what you're doing.

Empowering question:

What's one thing you've learned that would help you achieve your goals if you went over it one more time?

Meetings/Appointments	People to contact
Chores	Things to purchase

Distraction crusher

Additional notes (insights, lessons learned etc.)

Day 53

Date: _____

Don't let your learning lead to knowledge. Let your learning lead to action.

— JIM ROHN

Daily goals

-

-

-

-

-

-

Daily tip*: Maybe you don't know it.*

Are you struggling to get results yet find yourself saying, "Yeah, but I already know that" whenever someone gives you advice? If so, it's likely that you don't actually know it. Maybe you've been thinking more than doing. Is it possible that you haven't done everything necessary to master the skills you need? No amount of knowledge can make up for repetition. You can't truly know something until you actively participate in it. **If you don't live it, you don't know it.** That should be your motto!

Empowering question:

Can you identify at least one thing you thought you knew but realized you didn't?

Meetings/Appointments	People to contact
Chores	Things to purchase

Distraction crusher

Additional notes (insights, lessons learned etc.)

Day 54

Date: _____

The potential of the average person is like a huge ocean unsailed, a new continent unexplored, a world of possibilities waiting to be released and channeled toward some great good.

— BRIAN TRACY

Daily goals

-

-

-

-

-

-

Daily tip: *You can master any skill you want.*

I've said this before, but it's very true. Your ability to master something is more about your dedication and desire rather than your talent or when you started. If you're intensely passionate about it, you may even become one of the best at what you do.

Empowering question:

Do you believe you can master any skill you set your mind to? What exactly does that mean to you?

Meetings/Appointments	People to contact
Chores	Things to purchase

Distraction crusher

Additional notes (insights, lessons learned etc.)

Day 55

Date: _____

The most pathetic person in the world is someone who has sight but no vision.

— HELEN KELLER

Daily goals

-

-

-

-

-

-

Daily tip: *Always think long-term.*

What's your long-term vision of where you want to be 10 or 20 years from today? Whatever it is, focus on it as much as humanly possible. It's this vision that will allow you to stick with your goals no matter what. You can meet challenges head-on as long as you think of your vision, focus on the process, and stay patient. This is something every successful person goes through; you just have to ride it out until you get what you want.

Empowering question:

What happens when you visualize yourself having achieved your goal? How does it make you feel?

Meetings/Appointments	People to contact
Chores	Things to purchase

Distraction crusher

Additional notes (insights, lessons learned etc.)

Day 56

Date: _____

Success is a process, not an event.

— RICHIE NORTON

Daily goals

-

-

-

-

-

-

Daily tip: *Success is NOT an event.*

Success is a process that you'll have to go through. Once you've managed to have the success you want in one area of your life, you'll be able to replicate it in other areas. But you have to master the process first. The first step is to stop believing that success is an event that happens based on luck. You have to remind yourself that the journey towards your goals is an on-going process. It's something you have to go through for long-term results.

Empowering question:

Can you accept that the journey towards your goal is an on-going process that involves plenty of challenges and low points?

Meetings/Appointments	People to contact
Chores	Things to purchase

Distraction crusher

Additional notes (insights, lessons learned etc.)

STORY OF THE WEEK

Karoly Takacs – *Nothing can beat perseverance*

Karoly Takacs was a world-class pistol. After winning major national and international competitions, he dreamed of winning an Olympic Gold Medal at the 1940 Tokyo Olympic Games.

After joining the Hungarian Army, however, his dream was seemingly crushed. A faulty grenade exploded while training with his squad, resulting in severe injury to his right hand. No longer able to use his right hand, he had no hopes of making it to the Olympics, let alone winning anything.

When he showed up at the 1939 Hungarian National Pistol Shooting Championship, his colleagues were delighted to see him, complemented his courage, and thanked him for his willingness to come and cheer for them. You can imagine their surprise when he said he wasn't there to cheer for them, but to compete with them.

The amazing thing is that he didn't just compete. He *won* the competition! Sounds impossible, right? How could he compete if he couldn't use his right hand? The answer seems surprisingly simple: He used his left hand instead! As obvious as that might seem, it was harder than it sounds.

Despite the deep depression his accident caused, he managed to pull himself together. He decided to stop focusing on his loss and focus on what he still had: An exceptional mindset and a healthy left hand. He practiced diligently for a year without telling anyone. Perhaps he didn't feel like hearing people tell him to be "realistic" and give up his ridiculous dream of winning the Olympics and becoming the best shooter in the world.

Of course, Takacs pressed on, held onto his dream, and looked forward to the 1940 Olympics. Unfortunately, the 1940 Olympics were cancelled due to World War II. He pushed through his disappointment and began practicing for the 1944 Olympics. But they got cancelled, too!

Takacs continued training anyway and, in 1944, finally qualified for the 1948 London Olympics. He ultimately won a gold medal at age 38 and set a new world record in pistol shooting. Four years later, Takacs won the Gold Medal yet again at the 1952 Helsinki Olympics.

As this incredible story shows, being obsessed with a goal and persevering through hell and high water can lead to extraordinary results. To do this, we must develop an exceptional mindset and possess enough passion to push past great obstacles.

Monthly Goal Review ②

Congratulations! I'm so glad you made it this far. Make sure to celebrate this important milestone. You're already 60 days into your 90-day journey! You're definitely not a dabbler. If you're falling behind, do your best these last 30 days. Just imagine how proud you'll be of yourself when you achieve your goal in 30 days. Isn't that what you want?

Let's take some time to evaluate where you're at regarding the topics we covered this month:

- Turning your goal into an obsession
- Welcoming failure
- Beating Procrastination
- Adopting a Mastery Mindset

I'm going to ask you to rate yourself on a scale of 1 to 10 in each category. Again, be brutally honest with yourself. It's for you, not for me.

Turning your goal into an obsession – Are you really obsessed with your goal? How often do you think about it?

Your score:

Welcoming failure – To what extent do you fear failure?

Your score:

Beating procrastination – Do you do what you say you'll do, or do you frequently procrastinate?

Your score:

Adopting a Mastery Mindset – Are you using everything you learn? Are you really going deep with your goal? Or are you being superficial and jumping from one thing to another?

Your score:

At the end of the 90 days, I'll ask you to evaluate rate yourself one more time.

My Weekly Goals

My ONE Daily Habit

This is the one habit you'll stick to every day this week (and likely beyond) until you reach your goal.

-

My 3 Core Tasks

These are your most important tasks of the week. They all relate to your 90-Day Goal, and you'll do whatever it takes to achieve them this week.

-

-

-

Other tasks to accomplish (may or may not be related to your goal)

-

-

-

-

-

-

-

LESSON 9

INVESTING IN YOURSELF

The best investment you can make is not in stocks or real estate, it's in yourself! No investment can compete with a return on the time and money you put into yourself. In this lesson, we're going to discuss why it's so crucial to invest in yourself. We'll also cover the reasons you're likely to undervalue yourself.

How much do you value your time?

Have you ever calculated how much an hour of your time is worth? Is it $10? $100? $1,000? In truth, most people have no idea how much an hour of their time is worth. It's something that few people consider. Successful people know very well what their time is worth. They're also careful not to waste it. They know that time is more valuable money. After all, you can always earn more money, but you can never buy back time.

On the contrary, unsuccessful people tend to waste an incredible amount of time. They may watch TV for several hours a day, play video games excessively, or spend every weekend partying. This stems primarily from the fact that they don't realize how valuable their time is. Now, let's look at a few concrete examples of devaluing your time:

- Spending hours online to find coupons that save a few dollars

- Waiting in line for hours to buy the latest gadget
- Driving an extra 30 minutes to save a few bucks on a product
- Spending countless hours online looking for free information

Are these activities a good use of your time? If you devote hours on end to finding coupons, what does that say about how you value your time? An hour of your time is probably worth more than the money you'll save from coupons. If you could get a second job that would allow you to earn more money than you save during that time, you're technically losing money.

But what about looking for free information online? Sounds like a great idea, right? Not all free stuff is bad, and it has its uses, but you have to remember that nothing is truly free. Free resources have their price, and you need to realize when it's not worth it. Here are some potential costs that come with free information:

- We tend to undervalue things we get for free, and we aren't as motivated to make use of them. As a result, people often neglect to take action on free information. Worse still, a lot of it fails to sink in in the first place. Once that happens, you become little more than an information junkie.
- In small doses, free information has its benefits. If you're trying to consume it in large doses, however, you'd be better off buying a book, taking a class, or investing in the services of someone who can teach you what you need to know. Otherwise, you'll get lost in a sea of information. It's the internet--- there's no end to what you can find. It'll take hours just to make sense of the information, to say nothing of the time you'll spend organizing it into something user-friendly.
- The quality of the information will be inconsistent, meaning that some of what you find will be of lower quality than what you'd find in something you actually pay for.

All of this results in an inefficient use of your time and will usually bring subpar results. Again, I'm not saying free stuff has no value. I consume plenty of free resources myself. But when it comes to something I'm serious about, these are the reasons I prefer to invest money. It saves me time and effort, and is one of the ways in which I value myself.

Figuring out what your time is worth

You need to know how much your time is actually worth before you can properly value it. Below is a great exercise from millionaire mentor Dan Lok to calculate how much you should value an hour of your time:

1. Define your target, or rather, how much money you'd like to earn each month. For example's sake, let's say that you want to earn $10,000 a month.
2. Plug in the number of hours you work per month (let's say 150), and assume that you're productive for only half those hours. Dan Lok says that just one-third of our work hours are actually productive, but I'll be generous with you.
3. Plug these numbers into the following formula: The Amount of Money You Wish to Earn/ (The Number of Hours You Work/2) = What Your Time is Worth. When using the numbers in the example, the formula would look like this: $10,000/ (150 h/2) = $133. This would mean that your time is worth $133 per hour.

And there you have it! That's how much your time is worth. Of course, it may take a while before you're earning the amount of money necessary to reach your financial target. That's okay, however, because simply reminding yourself of how much your time is worth will allow you to value your time (and yourself!) more. As a result, you'll always be looking for ways to heighten your productivity and increase your hourly wage.

If you're earning $30 per hour but know you need an hourly wage of $133 to reach your monthly target of $10,000, your outlook will change. You'll spend more time on your most productive tasks. You'll also try to increase your efficiency by delegating or outsourcing any tasks that aren't worth $133 per hour. What can you do *right now* to increase your productivity per hour?

Invest in yourself

I enjoy reading books, so I tend to buy a lot of them. Despite this, it used to be difficult for me to invest in more expensive products. Nowadays, I don't have an issue buying books, courses, and other resources that are a little on the expensive side. This change stemmed from my increased ability to understand their value in terms of the results I get and the time I save.

I've seen a lot of people balk at the idea of investing just a few dollars in a book. An unwillingness to invest in yourself is a huge sign that you don't value yourself properly. Worse still, it's going to cost you a lot of money in the long-run. By this, I mean the money you could've earned if you'd put more into what you were doing. If you want to be successful, you have to adopt the behaviors of successful people. These people are constantly learning and aren't afraid to spend thousands of dollars a year on things that will help them learn more and achieve bigger things. Now, I know that a lot of people don't have thousands of dollars to spend in that way. But if you're reading and relating to this book, it's highly likely that you can invest in something, even if it's small. I find it ironic that those who seem to need the least amount of help tend to invest in themselves the most.

Why invest in courses, books, and the like?

Here are a few reasons to invest in these things:

1. **They significantly shorten your learning curve–** Why try to learn something by yourself when you can get help from people who have extensive experience with it? Taking advantage of this can save you months and even years of time. And as we've learned by now, time is money!
2. **They provide a clear structure that's easy to follow** – You don't want to spend hours gathering information to "create" your own course. Letting a course, book, or other resource take care of the structure is far easier. It frees up your mind and time so you can focus on learning and taking consistent action.
3. **They strengthen your belief that what you want is possible** –

If you buy a great course from someone who already possesses the skills you want, it makes it easier to believe that you can achieve what they have.

4. **They force you to put more skin in the game** – If you spend $300 on something, you'll be more motivated to put it to use than you would if you'd gotten it for free. I struggled for a long time to create a morning ritual, and I couldn't make it stick until I invested in a program for it. I've had a daily morning ritual for quite some time now, and the program was less than $40. I think this is one of the main reasons that people spend so much money on things like coaching.

Selecting the right course

You may be worried about scams, and they are plentiful. That said, there are also many great courses that deliver excellent results if you truly commit to them. The following tips can help you avoid the bad stuff and find something amazing:

- **Never buy a course from someone who isn't living what they're teaching.** It sounds obvious, but it begs repeating. You want to make sure the creator of the course has solid credentials and knows exactly what they're talking about.
- **Look for products with a money-back guarantee.** This isn't a must, per se, but it's a sign that the creator is serious about their product.
- **Never buy on the spot.** Anyone with a good sense of marketing will try to create a sense of urgency and encourage you to make an immediate purchase. The urgency is just a marketing tool, however. You'll almost always be able to by the product at a later date. No matter how tempting it is to buy instantly, resist the urge. Give yourself some time to think. This is especially important if you feel hesitant to begin with. When in doubt, wait it out.
- **Calculate your potential return on the investment** – Calculate the minimum amount of time you'll save and how much money you're likely to earn/preserve in the long-run. Be conservative.

Include non-monetary benefits as well, such as peace of mind. These benefits are subjective, so it's your job to determine the monetary value you give them. Once you've figured out these variables, you can make an informed decision on whether to buy the course.

How to make the most of a program:

Now, let's have a look at how you can make the most of the resources you invest in and ensure your money is well spent.

1. **Commit and give it your all.** Once you buy a program, book, or another self-help tool, go all-in. Maintain a mindset that says, "I will squeeze out every ounce of value I can from this! I'll do everything I can to get more than what I invested!"
2. **Take action on everything you learn.** Never assume that you already know something unless you've done it repeatedly. Look at it this way: If even one person got great results from the program you're using, you can keep learning until you get them, too.
3. **Master the fundamentals.** In addition to accepting the fact that you probably don't know as much as you think you do, you need to be willing to make changes and try new things. Go through the content until you master it, no matter how long it takes. If you don't get the results you expect, just ask yourself, "Am I missing something here? Have I *really* tried everything?"
4. **Focus on one book, course, etc. before moving to another one.** Don't be a dabbler that takes course after course or reads book after book without getting significant results. Focus on one thing at a time and resist the urge to work on all aspects of your life simultaneously.
5. **Be consistent.** Make sure you take some kind of action each day. When you feel depressed, tired, or discouraged, focus on doing minor tasks to maintain momentum until your motivation returns.
6. **Be patient.** No matter what you want to change in your life, it's going to take time. Be patient and have faith in the process. If

you're trying to make major, long-term changes in your life (like losing weight or starting a business), give yourself at *least* 2 to 3 years to do get it done. Then, make it your daily focus.

A final piece of advice I would like to give you is to invest before you are ready. Is there a course you know you could benefit from now but aren't planning to buy for another few months? If you've got the money for it now and know you'll buy it in the future, just do it now. Why delay the benefits if there's nothing to stop you from starting now? This holds particularly true if the purchase is something that could help your business.

So, if you want to set exciting goals and actually achieve them you can buy my course for only.... No, I'm just kidding.

Day 57

Date: _____

> *Learn to work harder on yourself than you do on your job. If you work hard on your job you can make a living. If you work hard on yourself, you can make a fortune.*

— JIM ROHN

Daily goals:

-

-

-

-

-

-

Daily tip: *Invest in yourself because no one else will.*

If you don't invest in yourself, nobody else will. In the rare instance that someone else does invest in you (like your company, for instance), it will be with the intention of enabling you to make more money for them. They aren't trying to help you make more money for yourself. No one can help you become a better person but you. Few people, if any, will sincerely encourage you to follow your dream and become the person you must be to achieve it. Bottom-line: Make sure you invest in yourself!

Empowering question

What is the one skill that, if developed, would have the most impact on your life?

Meetings/Appointments	People to contact
Chores	Things to purchase

Distraction crusher

Additional notes (insights, lessons learned etc.)

Day 58

Date: _____

The difference between successful people and really successful people is that really successful people say no to almost everything.

— WARREN BUFFET

Daily goals:

-

-

-

-

-

-

Daily tip: *Learn to say no.*

Valuing yourself and your time means that you have to say no to things that aren't the best use of your time. Your time is extremely valuable and shouldn't be given recklessly. Each time you say yes to something that's out of line with your values, you miss an opportunity to focus on something meaningful. This could be spending time with your family or working on a major project. When you think of it this way, refusing to say "no" would be downright selfish.

Empowering question

What could you say "no" to in your life? What meaningful activity could you spend more time on?

Meetings/Appointments	People to contact
Chores	Things to purchase

Distraction crusher

Additional notes (insights, lessons learned etc.)

Day 59

Date: _____

Love yourself. Forgive yourself. Be true to yourself. How you treat yourself sets the standard for how others will treat you.

— STEVE MARABOLI

Daily goals:

-

-

-

-

-

-

Daily tip: *Valuing your time is valuing yourself.*

Valuing and making effective use of your time is about more than your productivity. Valuing your time means respecting and valuing yourself enough to use your time wisely. In short, productivity isn't just about getting things done, it's about respecting yourself and building self-esteem. Stop giving your time to every single person who asks for it. Your time is not free!

Empowering question

How could making better use of your time help you respect yourself more?

Meetings/Appointments	People to contact
Chores	Things to purchase

Distraction crusher

Additional notes (insights, lessons learned etc.)

Day 60

Date: _____

I will take care of me for you, if you will take care of you for me.

— JIM ROHN

Daily goals:

-

-

-

-

-

-

Daily tip: *Refusing to invest in yourself is selfish.*

If you aren't developing yourself and learning new skills, you're doing a great disservice to those around you. It's only when you take care of yourself that you can offer something to others. When you have poor self-discipline, low self-esteem, or a lack of purpose in life, you're not the only one who suffers. Your kids, partner, family, or friends (basically everyone around you) suffer as well. So, isn't taking good care of yourself one of the best things you can do for them?

Empowering question

In which areas of your life are you "being selfish" by not improving yourself?

Meetings/Appointments	People to contact
Chores	Things to purchase

Distraction crusher

Additional notes (insights, lessons learned etc.)

Day 61

Date: _____

Most people died at 25 and aren't buried until they're 75.

Daily goals:

-

-

-

-

-

-

Daily tip: *Do you want to be where you are now in 20 years?*

Most people stop growing once they reach adulthood. They hold the same thoughts and beliefs for decades. They stop questioning the world because they see no need to do so. Their way of thinking has gotten them by for many years, so it must be accurate, right? Anything that's too different from their thought processes is probably wrong, anyway. They act as if they've reached their full potential when it couldn't be further from the truth. How about you? Are you reinventing yourself on a regular basis? Are you continuously learning and pushing yourself, or are you the same person you were 5 years ago?

Empowering question

How much have you changed in the past 6 months? How about the past year? What about the last 5 years? Would someone who hasn't seen you in a couple of years notice a difference?

Meetings/Appointments	People to contact
Chores	Things to purchase

Distraction crusher

Additional notes (insights, lessons learned etc.)

Day 62

Date: _____

> *Your life has nothing to do with you. It is about everyone whose life you touch and how you touch it.*

— Neale Donald Walsch

Daily goals:

-

-

-

-

-

-

Daily tip: *The Golden rule of personal development.*

In my opinion, there's only one rule you absolutely need in life, and that's making sure that people are better off after having met you. In short, are you making a positive impact on each person you encounter? This means everyone from friends, family, and colleagues to the cashier at the grocery store or your waitress at a restaurant. If you aren't making a positive impact, why? If you make a sincere effort to live by this rule, you won't need many others.

Empowering question

What impact are you having on the people around you? What concrete changes have you witnessed in those who spend a lot of time with you?

Meetings/Appointments	People to contact
Chores	Things to purchase

Distraction crusher

Additional notes (insights, lessons learned etc.)

Day 63

Date: _____

Be yourself; everyone else is already taken.

— OSCAR WILDE

Daily goals:

-

-

-

-

-

-

Daily tip*: "Just" be yourself!*

How often have you been told to "just be yourself"? Quite annoying, isn't it? It's hard to be yourself in a world that's constantly trying to turn you into someone else. Are you really living the life *you* want? Or are you simply doing what those around you say you should do? You know deep down what you should be doing, but you can't do much about it until you trust yourself.

Empowering question

Who are you and what do you want from life?

Meetings/Appointments	People to contact
Chores	Things to purchase

Distraction crusher

Additional notes (insights, lessons learned etc.)

STORY OF THE WEEK

Bruce Lee – *A spiritual force greater than faith*

In January of 1969, 28-year-old Bruce Lee was a minor TV star in the United States. He was a father of two at the time and had little financial security. It was at this time that he wrote the following mission statement:

SECRET My Definite Chief Aim I, Bruce Lee, will be the first highest paid Oriental super star in the United States. In return I will give the most exciting performances and render the best of quality in the capacity of an actor. Starting 1970 I will achieve world fame and from then onward till the end of 1980 I will have in my possession $10,000,000. I will live the way I please and achieve inner harmony and happiness. Bruce Lee Jan. 1969

Amazingly, Bruce Lee managed to achieve all of this before dying at age 32. Writing your goals down won't automatically make them, of course. But it starts the process and helps you crystallize your thoughts and bring your intentions into the real world. Bruce Lee mastered his mind by developing an unshakeable confidence that, in his own words, went beyond even faith.

"I feel I have this great creative and spiritual force within me that is greater than faith, greater than ambition, greater than confidence, greater than determination, greater than vision. It is all these combined. My brain becomes magnetized with this domination force which I hold in my hand." – Bruce Lee

What about you? What will you do to create an unshakeable confidence in your vision?

Weekly Goal Review – week 9

Congratulations! You've made it through the ninth week. I think now is a good time to repeat a Jim Rohn quote I mentioned a few days ago: Learn to work harder on yourself than you do on your job, if you work hard on your job you can make a living, if you work hard on yourself you can make a fortune.

Whether you make a fortune or not depends on your preferences and goals. Yet working hard on yourself will yield results that benefit both you and those around you.

But enough lecturing, let's see how much progress you've made with your goals.

What went well:

What you could have done better:

Let's look at the progress you made regarding your limiting beliefs and any other obstacles that stand in your way.

What went well:

What I could have done better:

If you've discovered any new limiting beliefs, write them down below, along with what you'll do to overcome them. Otherwise, write down your previous limiting beliefs and what you'll do to continue working on them:

My Weekly Goals

My ONE Daily Habit

This is the one habit you'll stick to every day this week (and likely beyond) until you reach your goal.

-

My 3 Core Tasks

These are your most important tasks of the week. They all relate to your 90-Day Goal, and you'll do whatever it takes to achieve them this week.

-

-

-

Other tasks to accomplish (may or may not be related to your goal)

-

-

-

-

-

-

-

LESSON 10

GETTING RESULTS THROUGH MASSIVE ACTION

Do you know why most people fail? It's actually very simple: They don't take enough action! Nobody wants to hear that, of course, so people keep looking for quick tips. "You need to take more action, Thibaut". Yes, I know, but let me watch this YouTube video really quick, it sounds really informative. Oh, and I also need to read this book over here. Oh, and that other one as well...

What massive action really is

As I mentioned earlier, society has conditioned you to think a little is a lot, thus leading you to take little action yet expect big results. There is a major problem with that: because you think you're working hard, you get really frustrated when you go months without changes. Then, you start getting irritated by successful people who seem luckier and smarter than you, which ultimately leads you to give up.

Have you considered the possibility that you just weren't doing what it took to achieve the results you wanted? Is it possible that you underestimated the amount of time and work required to get results?

Forget for a moment what most people consider hard work and ask yourself the following questions:

- What does giving my absolute best look like?
- How much more could I promote myself?
- How many more clients could I contact?
- How much more could I practice my skills?

Doing this will enable you to realize that you could probably do a lot more than you are.

Lack of patience is killing you

The media isn't doing you any favors. Marketers are constantly bombarding you with false messages. They want you to believe that making money is easy or that you can lose large amounts of weight in just a couple of weeks. Then, when you fail to get the results their products promise, your self-esteem takes a hit. Feeling bad about yourself isn't conducive to success, and ultimately leads to giving up.

Patience is one of the greatest skills you can develop. Success never happens overnight, but it will come if you take massive action and learn to persist long enough. Remember, success is a process not an event.

You don't need more knowledge

For most people, lack of knowledge isn't an issue. Chances are they already know what they should be doing. Reading books or going to seminars is often just a way to procrastinate and avoid taking real action. You learn 10 times more by doing something than by reading about it.

There's a huge difference between thinking you know something and actually knowing something. You can only truly know something by practicing it again and again until it becomes part of you. Then, it turns into a sort of intuitive knowledge. Instead of being something you know intellectually, it's something you're embodying.

You can read up on public speaking all you want, but your knowledge is useless if you've never made a speech. Similarly, you can't learn to drive a car by reading a book about it.

Each time you catch yourself thinking that you need to read another book, take another seminar, or watch another video, ask yourself how much action you're taking on the knowledge you've already accumulated. If it's not enough, you need to focus on action instead of knowledge.

You can't add value to anything without taking action

You may not feel like you have much to offer, and you may feel as if there's nothing you can teach others. There are two main reasons for this feeling.

1. You have absolutely nothing to teach (very unlikely).
2. You have a lot of knowledge that you're unaware of.

1. You have absolutely nothing to teach

Maybe you really don't know anything and can't add value to other people's lives in a way that you can monetize. Let's assume that's the case. Now, how hard is it to learn a new skill or acquire knowledge you can share and monetize? It's not as hard as you may think. Let's say there's a topic you know nothing about and have no particular interest in, but decide to study for some reason. You do some online research and identify three experts on the topic. Then you purchase their books and read them within the month. Keep in mind that these people have spent decades studying the topic and their books offer you a huge chunk of their knowledge. Once you've read the books and spent some time soaking up the information, how much more will you know than the average person? At this point, you'd probably know more on the topic than 90% of the population. So, after all of that, wouldn't you have something you could teach other people? Of course! And we're not even talking about a subject you enjoy. Can you imagine how much more you'd learn if you were researching a topic you were actually interested in? You probably already have something you're interested in and know a lot about. It's just a matter of realizing it.

The process above is more or less what I used when I published my first book on Amazon. I discovered the power of setting goals and decided to share it with other people. My book was well-received, so I figured I might as well keep learning about the topic and position myself as an expert.

Yet in the months before the release of my book, I didn't know much about setting goals. In fact, I had only started setting goals barely a year before releasing my book. That's when I started reading books from goal-setting experts like Jim Rohn and Brian Tracy. I also read the works of personal development experts like Steve Pavlina. I even read books by life coaches and hypnotherapists. All this so I could write a comprehensive guide that would focus on the mindset required to set and achieve exciting goals.

I didn't do anything special here. The key thing is that I was passionate about the topic. I went through the same process with habits and morning rituals. I learned about these topics, immediately put what I learned into practice, and started to share my experiences by writing books on both topics. Could other people do the same? Absolutely!

The point here is that you don't need 20 years of experience to acquire enough skills and knowledge to impact others. You just need the following 4 things:

1. More knowledge than most people on a particular topic (this is fairly easy to manage)
2. A passion for what you're learning
3. A willingness to take immediate action whether you're 100% ready or not (by the way, no one is ever 100% ready)
4. A willingness to learn how to effectively market yourself

You can add what you've learned in this planner to that list, too. And then you'll really make things happen!

2. You have a lot of knowledge you're unaware of

There's something in psychology called the "curse of knowledge". Things we know well eventually become so natural that we start believing everyone else knows them, too. We totally lose perspective on what the average person does and doesn't know. You've probably had conversations that made you suddenly realize how much you knew about something. Or perhaps you realized how little knowledge other people had about a specific topic.

Is there a topic you're currently passionate about? If so, it's likely that you know more about it than most people do. Thanks to the internet, a little creativity mixed with passion and perseverance is enough to make money from just about anything. If you want to make a living from your passion, brainstorm ways to do so on a daily basis.

Is luck real?

Someone who takes lots of action over a long period of time has a high chance of achieving their goals. Personally, I'm not a big believer in luck. As Thomas Jefferson said, "I'm a great believer in luck, and I find the harder I work the more I have of it."

Imagine you go from cold calling 10 people a day to 100. How much better are your chances of getting new clients? If, in addition to that, you decide to spend 30 minutes a day reading books about cold calling and sales, how much bigger is your chance of getting results? These things are just the tip of the iceberg. There are probably many other things you could do to improve your performance. You could, for instance, hire a coach or find a mentor.

Now take a look at your 90-Day Goal. Are you really doing everything you can to achieve it? Put yourself in someone else's shoes for a bit. If you looked at your actions from the outside, how much would you bet on your success? $100? $10,000? $100,000?

Day 64

Date: _____

> *If people knew how hard I worked to get my mastery, it wouldn't seem so wonderful at all.*
>
> — MICHELANGELO

Daily goals:

-

-

-

-

-

-

Daily tip: *Are you a master or a dabbler?*

Do you stick to something long enough to master it, or do you jump from one thing to another? Dabbling is one of the major reasons people fail to achieve their goals. If there's only one thing you remember from this planner, it should be to avoid dabbling at all costs. Stop blaming courses, books, teachers, or seminars. Instead, keep going back to basics until you master them. If other people get results, you can (and will), too. Stick with it!

Empowering question

What's one example in your life where you failed because you gave up too soon?

Meetings/Appointments	People to contact
Chores	Things to purchase

Distraction crusher

Additional notes (insights, lessons learned etc.)

Day 65

Date: _____

> *"Knowledge is power". It is nothing of the sort! Knowledge is only potential power. It becomes power only when, and if, it is organized into definite plans of action, and directed to a definite end.*
>
> — NAPOLEON HILL

Daily goals:

-

-

-

-

-

-

Daily tip: *Action over knowledge*

It's rare that you need more knowledge. Nine times out of 10, the only thing you need is more action. How much time do you spend taking real, concrete actions that genuinely move you towards your goal? You should spend 90% of your time taking action. The pursuit of knowledge is often a way to procrastinate on what you know you should be doing. It feels good and many of us enjoy it, but it doesn't produce results. A good mantra for you: Action! Action! Action!

Empowering question

If you could take just one action every day to move you closer to your goal, what would it be?

Meetings/Appointments	People to contact
Chores	Things to purchase

Distraction crusher

Additional notes (insights, lessons learned etc.)

Day 66

Date: _____

If what you are doing is not moving you towards your goals, then it's moving you away from your goals.

— BRIAN TRACY

Daily goals:

-

-

-

-

-

-

Daily tip: *Are you talking too much?*

A general rule is that the more you talk, the less you get done. As an introvert, I tend to think that most people talk too much. Talk is cheap. Many people like to talk about changing the world, but few are actually doing something about it. When you talk about your goal, it gives you a false sense of accomplishment that leads to nowhere. Be aware of that when you share your goals. Sharing your goals is a great way to create accountability, but it doesn't mean you should talk about them constantly. It's always better to do the hard work in silence than to talk about it all the time. Give it a try. I promise you'll get more done.

Empowering question

How much time do you spend working on your goals versus talking about them?

Meetings/Appointments	People to contact
Chores	Things to purchase

Distraction crusher

Additional notes (insights, lessons learned etc.)

Day 67

Date: _____

> *Most people fail only because they are operating at the wrong level of action.*
>
> — GRANT CARDONE

Daily goals:

-
-
-
-
-
-

Daily tip: *Your brain learns through action.*

Your brain learns by doing. It learns through experiments and so-called "failures", which are just feedback. Like I said earlier, you'll always learn 10 times more by doing something than by simply reading about it. You can't learn to drive a car, deliver a great speech, or play the piano just by reading about it! Prioritize massive action, especially at the beginning of your journey. Then, use books to perfect your craft and go to the next level.

Empowering question

What does massive action look like for you? What could you be doing 10 times more? What could you be doing 10 times less?

Meetings/Appointments	People to contact
Chores	Things to purchase

Distraction crusher

Additional notes (insights, lessons learned etc.)

Day 68

Date: _____

It's not knowing what to do; it's doing what you know.

— TONY ROBBINS

Daily goals:

-

-

-

-

-

-

Daily tip: *Turn your knowledge into experience.*

Train yourself to constantly take action on what you learn. Stop jumping from course to course. Make sure you master the content of a course through consistent practice before moving to something new. Piling up knowledge won't get results, but taking more action will. That's how you get tangible results.

Empowering question

What do you know intellectually that you haven't mastered on a deeper level? List at least 5 things

Meetings/Appointments	People to contact
Chores	Things to purchase

Distraction crusher

Additional notes (insights, lessons learned etc.)

Day 69

Date: _____

Whatever you're thinking, think bigger.

— TONY HSIEH

Daily goals:

-

-

-

-

-

-

Daily tip: *Maximize your goals by 10.*

Whatever you're thinking, think bigger. And bigger again! What is it you really want but haven't dared to dream of? Thinking bigger is important because it forces you to operate on an entirely different level of thinking. Most people think way too small. I'm amazed that some of the smartest people I know think way too small. Or at least I think so. Think of your ultimate goal or vision as a tool that will compel you to become more so you can achieve it. Even if you don't achieve it, it will force you to get out of your comfort zone. More importantly, it will really excite you because it's what you truly want, not some smaller goal you only kind of want because it's "realistic".

Empowering question

What's the biggest goal you can possibly imagine for yourself? How does it make you feel?

Meetings/Appointments	People to contact
Chores	Things to purchase

Distraction crusher

Additional notes (insights, lessons learned etc.)

Day 70

Date: _____

> *Work like hell. I mean you just have to put in 80 to 100 hour weeks every week. [This] improves the odds of success. If other people are putting in 40-hour work weeks and you're putting in 100-hour work weeks, then even if you're doing the same thing you know that... you will achieve in 4 months what it takes them a year to achieve.*
>
> — ELON MUSK

Daily goals:

-

-

-

-

-

-

Daily tip: *What is your definition of hard work?*

Sometimes, when creating a business, you'll have to work way beyond 40 hours per week. You may already have a full-time job, and will have to spend an extra 20-30 hours each week for a year or more to create your dream career and finally escape your 9-5 job. There's nothing wrong with that. Don't worry about what other people think of it. Let them go to jobs they hate and keep focusing on your goal. Let them party when you work, let them call you crazy or a workaholic. Jim Rohn said that "some people have so given up on life, they have joined the Thank God It's Friday Club." Make sure you don't end up being one of them. You can't just stay 40 years at a job you hate when you have something you're truly passionate about. Make it happen.

Empowering question

How can you maximize your odds of achieving your goals?

Meetings/Appointments	People to contact
Chores	Things to purchase

Distraction crusher

Additional notes (insights, lessons learned etc.)

STORY OF THE WEEK

Glenn Cunningham- *Your will is the strongest force there is*

Glenn Cunningham was destined to die. When he didn't, doctors said that he would never regain use of his legs. His amazing story comes courtesy of Bill Dubin.

In 1917, 8-year-old Cunningham was attending a school that used a coal stove for heat. He was tasked with coming to school early each day to use the kerosene to start the heater and ensure the room was warm by the time his teacher and classmates arrived. One of these days he found that someone had unintentionally put gasoline in the kerosene container. This led to a terrible fire that tore through the school and trapped him inside. Cunningham was ultimately rushed to the hospital, barely clinging to life. He had severe burns all over his lower body, and was just conscious enough to hear his doctor tell his mother that he was sure to die. The doctor went on to say that this was actually better than the alternative, because the fire had injured his body beyond repair. Clearly, the bedside manner of physicians has changed for the better over the past several decades.

Cunningham refused to accept this news and was determined to survive. To the amazement of the doctor, he did exactly that. Regaining the ability to walk was an impossibility, however, and the doctor insisted that he would spend the rest of his life without the use of his legs. Even so, his mother wouldn't let them amputate and he refused to believe their analysis of his fate. Once released from the hospital, however, Cunningham experienced a complete lack of mobility from the waist down.

His parents massaged his legs on a daily basis, but this did nothing to return his ability to feel and move them. This only increased his faith that he would walk again. Confined to a wheelchair, Cunningham threw himself onto the ground and dragged himself across his yard. He strained to pull himself up onto the fence and made his way across it, sincerely believing that he would learn to walk again. He was relentless in his efforts, and they paid off. Eventually, he regained the ability to stand. Standing turned into walking with the assistance of others, which gave way to walking on his own. This was the least of his accomplishments, however, because he eventually learned to run!

Cunningham began running virtually everywhere. He ultimately made the track team in college, and did so well that he earned the nickname "Kansas Flyer."

In February of 1934, he ran a mile in 4 minutes and 8 seconds, which was the fastest indoor mile. He cut another second off of his run during a prominent indoor race, and ran what was the world's fastest mile at that time. All this from a boy who had been destined to die and would never walk, let alone run.

In the end, Cunningham was inducted into the National Track and Field Hall of Fame in 1974.

Weekly Goal Review – week 10

Congratulations! You've completed the tenth week. If you're behind schedule, it's crucial to take some massive action in the few weeks you have left. Give it all you've got to ensure you achieve your goal by the 90-day mark. It's not over yet!

Now, let's evaluate your progress.

What went well:

What you could have done better:

Let's look at the progress you made regarding your limiting beliefs and any other obstacles that stand in your way.

What went well:

What I could have done better:

If you've discovered any new limiting beliefs, write them down below, along with what you'll do to overcome them. Otherwise, write down your previous limiting beliefs and what you'll do to continue working on them:

My Weekly Goals

My ONE Daily Habit

This is the one habit you'll stick to every day this week (and likely beyond) until you reach your goal.

-

My 3 Core Tasks

These are your most important tasks of the week. They all relate to your 90-Day Goal, and you'll do whatever it takes to achieve them this week.

-

-

-

Other tasks to accomplish (may or may not be related to your goal)

-

-

-

-

-

-

-

LESSON 11

IT ALL STARTS IN YOUR MIND

We're the only species on earth that has the power to turn thoughts into things, but few people realize what it means and how powerful it is. This goal-setting planner is the result of a thought. If I hadn't had the thought, cultivated it, and acted upon it, the planner wouldn't exist.

You have the incredible power to turn your thoughts into real things. Your thoughts are the most valuable asset you'll ever have. Everything human beings have created in this world began with thoughts. Your thoughts and your ability to turn them into unshakable beliefs will determine whether you achieve your goals. As such, they should be your main focus as you work on creating an extraordinary life.

As you become obsessed with a thought, it becomes part of your reality. Your subconscious mind starts to believe in it and looks for ways to make it happen. As you hold that thought longer and longer and with more frequency, it becomes a belief. When the belief becomes more prominent in your life, it will manifest in concrete actions. It is these actions that will produce tangible results in your life.

Whatever great goal you have must be in your thoughts for months, years, or even longer before it actually happens. You need to be prepared so you can seize opportunities the moment they arrive. If you want to be able to do this, you must constantly improve your ability to think, talk, and act as if you've already achieved your goals. You must accomplish it in your mind thousands of times with intense clarity until you're absolutely certain that it's going to happen.

If, for instance, you want to become CEO of a company, you should constantly be thinking of what you'd do if you were the CEO of that company. What would your hiring process be? What would the core value of your company be? How would you motivate your employees? What kind of corporate culture would you create? What would you do differently? What would your typical day look like? And so on. The more specific your thinking is, the more believable it will be.

Make it as real as possible

To strengthen your belief in your goals, you need to make them as real as possible. You can do this in a few different ways:

- **Learn as much as you can about your goal:** Study your goal as much as you can and immerse yourself in it.
- **Surround yourself with people who have already achieved it:** Seek out those who've already achieved your goals. Join groups or even hire a mentor or coach if you need to. The real value in doing that isn't in picking their brain but in absorbing their mindset. Being around them will significantly help you believe your goal is possible.
- **Each day, read books or watch videos about people who've achieved your goals:** If you have yet to find a way to physically surround yourself with people who have what you want, read books and watch videos to increase your understanding of how they think and behave.
- **Buy books, courses, etc. from people who've achieved your goals:** Buy the best resources you can find and go through them diligently. Go over them several times if you need to, just make sure you master the content and stick to it until you get results.
- **Talk as if you're absolutely certain you'll achieve your goal:** Train yourself to talk with more certainty. Remember Muhammad Ali? He referred to himself as the greatest long before he actually became one of the greatest boxers of all time.

The more you talk and write with certainty, using words like "I will", "definitely", and "absolutely", the more action you'll take. You can start by replacing expressions like "I'll try", "I may", and "maybe" with "I will" whenever possible. Do this both in what you say and what you write. See the section "words to ban from your vocabulary" for more information.

Now, let's begin the new week.

Day 71

Date: _____

We have to see ourselves there long before it happens.

Daily goals:

-

-

-

-

-

-

Daily tip: *Plant the seeds of success in your mind and water it every day.*

Have you heard the story of the Chinese bamboo? The Chinese bamboo must be watered every day in order to grow, yet it only starts growing in its fifth year! But when it does, do you know how fast it grows? It grows 90 feet in just 5 weeks. The same goes for many of our big goals and dreams. You might look at some overnight successes and think how lucky those people are. But I can almost guarantee they planted the seeds of success in their minds years before their goals became a reality. It was there years before it happened, even if few people could see it.

Empowering question

What seed could you start planting in your mind from this point on that you can water every day?

Meetings/Appointments	People to contact
Chores	Things to purchase

Distraction crusher

Additional notes (insights, lessons learned etc.)

Day 72

Date: _____

Create a vision for the life you really want and then work relentlessly towards making it a reality.

— ROY T. BENNETT

Daily goals

-

-

-

-

-

-

Daily tip: *No one else can see what you see.*

What's your vision for yourself? The bigger your goals, the less likely it is that those around you will support you. You may be the only one who believes in your goals and dreams, but that's all you need. In the end, the only thing that matters is whether YOU believe in your vision and give yourself permission to pursue it. As you strengthen your beliefs day after day, what other people think is realistic becomes increasingly irrelevant.

Empowering question

What vision do you have for yourself?

Meetings/Appointments	People to contact
Chores	Things to purchase

Distraction crusher

Additional notes (insights, lessons learned etc.)

Day 73

Date: _____

Nothing can change until we do. When we change our world will change.

— EARL NIGHTINGALE

Daily goals

-

-

-

-

-

-

Daily tip: *Everything you need is in your mind.*

Stop focusing on the outside world and learn to focus on your inner world instead. Everything in the outside world is a reflection of your inner world. As you continue working on the inside, your environment will change, either because your new attitudes and behavior will influence the people around you, or because your new point of view will attract new people in your life. When you change, the world around you does, too. You can be sure that, at some point, your inner work will start changing your environment.

Empowering question

What can you do to focus more on the inside? What does focusing on the inside really mean to you?

Meetings/Appointments	People to contact
Chores	Things to purchase

Distraction crusher

Additional notes (insights, lessons learned etc.)

Day 74

Date: _____

In reality, all men are sculptors, constantly chipping away the unwanted parts of their lives trying to create a masterpiece.

— EDDIE MURPHY

Daily goals

-
-
-
-
-
-

Daily tip: *Be a creator not a consumer.*

I think we spend too much time consuming and not enough time creating. We have a strong internal desire to express our creativity. This creativity can take countless shapes. It could be writing a book, designing clothes, or drawing. It could also be painting, building something, or starting a company. It could even be creating deeper and more meaningful relationships. What about you? How much time do you spend consuming books, television, and other content versus creating things?

Empowering question

What do you secretly want to create in your life?

Meetings/Appointments	People to contact
Chores	Things to purchase

Distraction crusher

Additional notes (insights, lessons learned etc.)

Day 75

Date: _____

Success does not require that you look out the window. It only requires that you look in the mirror.

— Eric Thomas

Daily goals

-

-

-

-

-

-

Daily tip: *Life is a mindset game.*

I like to think of life as a mindset game. Master your mind and you can have whatever you want. Let it master you and you'll continually suffer. The quality of your thoughts determines the quality of your life. Each time you fail to get the results you want, look within and ask yourself how your current thoughts and beliefs are preventing you from getting the results you want.

Empowering question

What are the thoughts that prevent you from having the life you want?

Meetings/Appointments	People to contact
Chores	Things to purchase

Distraction crusher

Additional notes (insights, lessons learned etc.)

Day 76

Date: _____

> *Don't be afraid of the space between your dreams and reality. If you can dream it, you can make it so.*

— Belva Davis

Daily goals

-

-

-

-

-

-

Daily tips: *Getting from point A to point B.*

In its simplest definition, achieving a goal is "just" about filling the gap between point A (where you are now) and point B (where you want to be). As you visualize yourself having already accomplished your goals, can you identify the skills, beliefs, and mindset you need to go from point A to B?

Empowering question

Visualize yourself as having accomplished your goal. How will you go from points A to B?

Meetings/Appointments	People to contact
Chores	Things to purchase

Distraction crusher

Additional notes (insights, lessons learned etc.)

Day 77

Date: _____

I visualize things in my mind before I have to do them. It's like having a mental workshop.

— JACK YOUNGBLOOD

Daily goals

-

-

-

-

-

-

Daily tip*: Don't forget to visualize yourself working on your goals.*

As you set your daily and weekly goals, get into the habit of visualizing yourself working on and completing them. Allow yourself to feel the emotions you'll feel after you complete your tasks, such as pride and confidence. This enhances your chance of accomplishing your tasks.

Empowering Question

Can you visualize yourself working on your goals and completing them?

Meetings/Appointments	People to contact
Chores	Things to purchase

Distraction crusher

Additional notes (insights, lessons learned etc.)

STORY OF THE WEEK

Dan Pena – *Written, reviewed, changed, and affirmed!*

Dan Pena is a businessman and a high-performance coach who gives the following advice on successful goal-setting:

Pena feels that goals should be written and reviewed often. He used to read his goals 2 times a day, along with a variety of inspiring affirmations. These days, he reads his goals on a monthly basis and reviews affirmations each night. He marks the completion of goals he's achieved and alters those not yet completed. He believes in the phenomenal power of ensuring affirmations are the first thing you see in the morning and the last thing you see before bed.

Forget time limits!

Most people suggest setting time limits, but Pena doesn't believe in this. He feels goals should be accomplished "as soon as humanly possible", which he shortens to ASAHP. To him, time constraints do more harm than good and involve bending to what the masses think. This rings true for many people. How about you?

Forget being "realistic"

According to Pena, being "realistic" stems from fear of failure. Yet playing it safe keeps people from taking risks, which dampens the drive to do everything possible to accomplish the goal. For him, being realistic stunts self-growth and keeps you from reaching your full potential.

Personal Goals

Pena has kept two sets of goals since 1976. The first consists of publicly discussed goals that might involve other people. The second are what Jim Newman referred to as "under the skin goals". These are extremely personal goals that are shared with very few, typically just your mentor and your spouse. These personal goals might feel embarrassingly intimate, but they're crucial to your success and wellbeing. If your partner is unsupportive, Pena suggests finding a new one. Yes, he's that serious about achieving goals! This may seem extreme, but Pena opines that most relationships, be they personal or professional, are destroyed by incompatible goals. For those with similar goals, differences in what you're willing to sacrifice can also destroy the relationship.

Family-oriented goals

Pena's family goals have been heavily dependent on his children. He says the majority of these goals should be created with the children. Kids are notorious for changing their goals (an interest in firefighting gives way to dreams of becoming a police officer, and next thing you know they want to be an astronaut!) Even so, getting children accustomed to setting goals will eventually lead to achieving them.

Pena's personal goals

Dan Pena's father had one goal for him, which was to keep him alive until he reached "the age of reason". Pena felt he lacked focus and worried that his life would be unfulfilling unless he took a risk. He did this by joining the army during the Vietnam War and eventually training to be an officer. He was elated when the U.S. Congress deemed him "an officer and a gentleman". It meant the achievement of an "under the skin goal" that he hadn't shared with anyone else.

Ultimately, Pena warns against listening to people who haven't achieved their goals. He also emphasizes the importance of aiming high, going beyond one's comfort zone, and pushing past low self-esteem.

Weekly Goal Review – week 11

Congratulations! You've finished the eleventh week. Can you see yourself at the 90-day mark with your goal achieved and a huge smile on your face? If you're behind, don't give up hope. You don't want to reach the end wishing you'd done more, so make sure you do your best no matter what.

Now, let's evaluate your progress.

What went well:

What you could have done better:

Let's look at the progress you made regarding your limiting beliefs and any other obstacles that stand in your way.

What went well:

What I could have done better:

If you've discovered any new limiting beliefs, write them down below, along with what you'll do to overcome them. Otherwise, write down your previous limiting beliefs and what you'll do to continue working on them:

My Weekly Goals

My ONE Daily Habit

This is the one habit you'll stick to every day this week (and likely beyond) until you reach your goal.

-

My 3 Core Tasks

These are your most important tasks of the week. They all relate to your 90-Day Goal, and you'll do whatever it takes to achieve them this week.

-

-

-

Other tasks to accomplish (may or may not be related to your goal)

-

-

-

-

-

-

-

LESSON 12

REDESIGNING YOUR ENVIRONMENT FOR MAXIMUM EFFECTIVENESS

The best indicator of success is your environment. Your environment includes the people you interact with, what you're consuming from TV, radio, and news sources, and the neighborhood you live in, among other things. These things have a big influence on you because they shape your entire belief system. They shape your vision of the world. Imagine living with someone that's constantly telling you your dreams are impossible, you can't have the career you want, or you can't make the amount of money you want. Perhaps you don't even have to imagine this because you've lived with it. In which case you know how hard it would be to get where you want to be in that environment.

Now, imagine yourself being surrounded by people who've already achieved the goals you're working on. Spending time with them constantly reminds you that what you want is possible. It will eventually feel normal and natural. If all your friends are millionaires, wouldn't you say you have a better chance of becoming one yourself? Sure, these friends probably have connections that could be useful and maybe they'll lend you money. But that's not what I'm talking about. The real value in hanging around millionaires is the mindset it will enable you to develop. On a subconscious level, you'll pick up their beliefs, their body language, and their confidence. You'll begin to believe that you can do it, too.

Whatever your goal may be, you want to constantly remind yourself that it's possible. If you can't find a mentor or friends who can help you get there, you can find a virtual mentor. This can be done by readings books written by successful people, watching videos on YouTube, or taking courses and seminars. The more time you can spend with people who have what you want, the better.

The dangers of toxic people

I tend to be extremely selective with the people I hang out with. I can't deliberately spend time with people who tell me what I can or can't accomplish or try to demotivate me with negative comments. As I mentioned earlier in this planner, what they see as "realistic" isn't what I see as "realistic", nor is it what I want for myself. I don't need them to impose their model of reality on me, especially if it's a disempowering one.

Dealing with toxic people

I encourage you to spend time with people who believe in you and inspire you to be all that you can be. If the people around you aren't supportive, you might have to make some difficult decisions.

Unfortunately, there's no magic pill to get rid of toxic people in your life. There are only 3 options available:

1. Trying to convince them to get on board

2. Reducing how much time you spend with them

3. Not seeing them whatsoever.

1. Trying to convince them to get on board

The first thing you can do with people who aren't supportive of your goals and aspirations is to explain why what you're doing is important to you. You can then tell them why you want their full support. You can tell them how much their support matters and how it makes you feel when they're being negative. This approach may work with some people, but for many it won't. Trying to change someone's attitude and mindset is no easy task. It's much easier to change your own attitude and mindset.

2. Reducing how much time you spend with them

While it may be difficult to cut off close friends or relatives, you always have the option to spend less time with them. This may come handy if they're constantly trying to sabotage your efforts. Most people like the status quo and are terrified of change. Not only do they not want to change, they also don't want you to change. They already have a mental picture of who you're supposed to be and how you're supposed to behave. When you make major changes in your life, you threaten their little world, which may trigger their defense mechanism. If you can't reduce the amount of time spent with toxic people, you can avoid talking about your goals or anything else you know they'll laugh at, dismiss, or get sarcastic about.

3. Not seeing them whatsoever.

This is a very radical solution, but it's necessary in some cases. It may sound harsh, but if someone who says they're your "friend" constantly puts you down and impedes your progress, I don't see how they could really be your friend. People who truly care about you will support your decisions even if they disagree with them.

Further reducing your exposure to negativity

Another issue is the media. It constantly bombards us with negative news and, whether you know it or not, has a major impact on your mindset and beliefs. The use of fear is a powerful way to manipulate consumers. It's an easy way to rally them to a certain cause or entice them to buy a specific product. Our survival mechanism, which is designed to identify any potential threats, only makes this worse. Have you noticed how you're never attractive enough, smart enough, or rich enough? Or how war and natural disasters are rampant?

Whether the world is better or worse than it used to be is an irrelevant argument, because debating it won't change anything. Improving yourself and positively impacting as many people as possible is what creates change. Knowing more about all the terrible events taking place around the world won't make you a more compassionate person.

Spending hours in a café with your friends talking about how you're going to change the world isn't going to help, either.

Your job is to become the best version of yourself. Then you can positively impact the world. But you have to stay positive and believe that it's possible. And what will help you do that? Your environment, of course!

Day 78

Date: _____

Let your friends, family, and work associates know that you treat average like a terminal disease.

— Grant Cardone

Daily goals

-

-

-

-

-

Daily tip: *You are the product of your environment.*

Your environment can make or break you. You should constantly work on improving your environment by surrounding yourself with great people that already have what you want. Ideally, you'll want them to be your friends or your mentors. If that's not possible, read books and watch videos from people who already have what you want. Learn as much as you can from them, then take action!

Empowering question

What is the one thing you could do today to create a more positive and empowering environment?

Meetings/Appointments	People to contact
Chores	Things to purchase

Distraction crusher

Additional notes (insights, lessons learned etc.)

Day 79

Date: _____

You are the average of the five people you spend the most time with.

— JIM ROHN

Daily goals:

-

-

-

-

-

-

Daily tip: *Are your friends dragging you down?*

Are you currently hanging out with the right people? If you keep your current circle of friends, how likely are you to be where you want 10 years from now? You want to make sure you surround yourself with people who believe in you. The people you're closest to should want you to be your best.

Empowering question

Who is the one person you know that would have the most impact on your life if you spent more time with them?

Meetings/Appointments	People to contact
Chores	Things to purchase

Distraction crusher

Additional notes (insights, lessons learned etc.)

Day 80

Date: _____

You are a product of your environment. So choose the environment that will best develop you toward your objective. Analyze your life in terms of its environment. Are the things around you helping you toward success - or are they holding you back?

— W. Clement Stone

Daily goals

-

-

-

-

-

-

Daily tip: *The weaker your "why", the more your environment matters.*

If you have a strong "why" and a compelling vision, you're likely to keep moving forward even in a subpar environment. Eventually, you'll find yourself in a more positive environment. Without a compelling vision, however, you'll struggle to reach your goals in the face of an unfavorable environment. Strengthen your "why" and become bigger than your environment.

Empowering question

Are your goals clear and compelling enough to help you thrive in a challenging environment?

Meetings/Appointments	People to contact
Chores	Things to purchase

Distraction crusher

Additional notes (insights, lessons learned etc.)

Day 81

Date: _____

When your values are clear to you, making decisions becomes easier.

— ROY E. DISNEY

Daily goals

-

-

-

-

-

-

Daily tip: *You vs. Your environment. And the winner is...*

Are you influencing your environment or is your environment influencing you? If you're constantly impacted by your environment and the people around you, you may not be clear enough on your values. Once you know what you stand for, it becomes easy to make the right decisions. You'll know your boundaries and what you are and aren't willing to do. When this happens, outside factors will have less of an effect.

Empowering question

Are you influencing people around you, or are you the one being influenced?

Meetings/Appointments	People to contact
Chores	Things to purchase

Distraction crusher

Additional notes (insights, lessons learned etc.)

Day 82

Date: _____

A strong, successful man is not the victim of his environment. He creates favorable conditions.

— ORISON SWETT MARDEN

Daily goals

-
-
-
-
-
-

Daily tip: *Design your environment to maximize your chance of success.*

How can you make it easier to achieve your goals? What would you need, exactly? A quiet place you can work from? A clean desk? A faster computer? Courses that will save you time and enhance your focus? A support group?

It's important to build a strong foundation you can rely on while working on your goals. It might mean spending hours automating certain processes or thinking of ways to delegate certain tasks. You may also have to invest some time and money in the things you'll need. It will be more than worth it, however, because favorable environments intensify progress.

Empowering question

What would your ideal environment look like? What actions will you take to design it?

Meetings/Appointments	People to contact
Chores	Things to purchase

Distraction crusher

Additional notes (insights, lessons learned etc.)

Day 83

Date: _____

Show me your friends and I'll show you your future.

— MARK AMBROSE

Daily goals

-

-

-

-

-

-

Daily tip: *Who is your role model?*

It will be easier to achieve your goals if you can find good role models. These role models can be found online or in certain communities. It's extremely important to spend time surrounding yourself with people you want to be influenced by. This will have a positive impact on who you are and make it easier to believe in your goals.

Empowering Question

Where can you find role models you resonate with?

Meetings/Appointments	People to contact
Chores	Things to purchase

Distraction crusher

Additional notes (insights, lessons learned etc.)

Day 84

Date: _____

Surround yourself with those who only lift you higher.

— OPRAH WINFREY

Daily goals

-

-

-

-

-

-

Daily tip: *Show me your friends and I'll show you your future.*

Make sure you surround yourself with people who will regularly push and challenge you. Ideally, you want to be around people who are more successful than you. These are the people who will show you what's possible. They'll shatter your limiting beliefs and force you to raise your standards. They'll push you to become the person you must be to achieve your goals.

Empowering question

What's one small thing you can do every day to raise your standards?

Meetings/Appointments	People to contact
Chores	Things to purchase

Distraction crusher

Additional notes (insights, lessons learned etc.)

STORY OF THE WEEK

Cliff Young - *The tortoise and the hare*

Every year, Australia hosts a 543.7-mile endurance race from Sydney to Melbourne. This race, which takes five days to complete, is considered one the world's most grueling ultra-marathons. Its competitors are typically world-class athletes backed by large companies like Nike. The vast majority are under 30.

In 1983, a man named Cliff Young showed up to the race. He was 61-years-old and wore overalls and work boots. The crowd was shocked when he picked up a race number and join the other runners. The press and Young's fellow runners became curious and questioned him. They labeled him crazy and insisted there was no way he could finish the race. Young explained that he grew up on a farm that couldn't afford horses and tractors, and would sometimes spend 2 to 3 days running after and rounding up sheep. He felt this experience had given him the necessary skills to win.

At first, the other runner's left Young in their dust. The crowds and television audiences were amused because, as far as they could tell, Young didn't even run properly. He shuffled instead, and some people actually feared for his safety. At the time, those who ran the race believed that completing it meant running 18 hours per day and sleeping for 6.

Mathematically speaking, this is accurate, but Young had a better idea. On the second day, spectators got two big surprises: Young was still in the race, and had in fact been jogging all night.

When asked about his tactics for the rest of the race, Young claimed he would finish the race without sleeping. This was deemed impossible by everyone else, but he kept running. Every night brought him closer to those nearing the finish line. By the last night, he was ahead of all the young athletes he was competing against. He placed first in the race and set a new record for speed.

When awarded the 1st place prize of $10,000, Young said he was previously unaware of the prize money and hadn't entered for the money. He gave the entirety of his prize to several other runners, an act that endeared him to all of Australia.

In the following year, Young took 7th place in the same race, despite suffering a displaced hip along the way. In 1997, Young attempted to raise money for homeless children by running the length of Australia's border. He completed 4,051 miles of the 9,941-mile run, pulling out only because his lone crewmember became ill. He was 76-years-old.

Young passed away in 2003 at the age of 81, but his legacy lives on. Today, the "Young-shuffle" is considered the most energy-efficient running technique, and it's used by most ultra-marathoners. At least three winners of the Sydney to Melbourne race have used the shuffle to win the race, and today's competitors don't sleep during it. They feel that winning requires you to run all day and all night, just like Cliff Young did.

Weekly Goal Review – week 12

Congratulations! You've finished the twelfth week. Just one more week to go. Give it your best.

Now, let's evaluate your progress.

What went well:

What you could have done better:

Let's look at the progress you made regarding your limiting beliefs and any other obstacles that stand in your way.

What went well:

What I could have done better:

If you've discovered any new limiting beliefs, write them down below, along with what you'll do to overcome them. Otherwise, write down your previous limiting beliefs and what you'll do to continue working on them:

My Weekly Goals

My ONE Daily Habit

This is the one habit you'll stick to every day this week (and likely beyond) until you reach your goal.

-

My 3 Core Tasks

These are your most important tasks of the week. They all relate to your 90-Day Goal, and you'll do whatever it takes to achieve them this week.

-

-

-

Other tasks to accomplish (may or may not be related to your goal)

-

-

-

-

-

-

-

LESSON 13

WRAPPING UP

In this final lesson, I'd like to briefly go over everything we learned in this planner. To that end, let me remind you of the key concepts that will help you achieve your goals in the future.

Resourcefulness Over Resources

It doesn't matter what skills you need to develop or the resources you must acquire to achieve your goals. You already have everything you need within you. You don't need more resources; you need to learn how to become more resourceful. That will enable you to become the kind of person who attracts the resources you need.

You Create Your Life

The belief systems society imposes on you have nothing to do with reality. You don't need to buy into what the world tells you. You don't need to "be realistic". You have the ability to create a powerful belief system that will support you in achieving your current goals. It's your job to design the reality that leads to the results you desire.

Harsh Reality Acceptance

Success isn't what marketers would have you believe. There's no get-rich-quick scheme that will turn you into a millionaire in 30 days. There's no magic pill that will make you lose 50 pounds without exercising or modifying your diet. These are recipes for a mediocre life. Stop looking for shortcuts and accept the harsh reality of hard work. It's the only way to achieve the level of success you want.

Process-Based Thinking

Success is a process, not an event. It's the repetition of specific tasks each and every day that lead you to achieve your goals. Forget about the results and train yourself to focus on the process, i.e. what you do each day. Stop worrying about the future and focus on the present moment. If you do everything you can today, you'll eventually become your best self.

The Bullet-Proof Timeline

The bullet-proof timeline is your ticket out of Shiny Object Syndrome, which will kill your dreams if left unaddressed. Deciding on a bullet-proof timeline to focus on your goal enables you to persevere until you get what you want. Don't ever give up before your deadline. And remember, you'll have to remind yourself to stay patient many times.

The Mastery Mindset

Knowledge is power, but only if it's followed by consistent action. Constant repetition and immediate action is the only way to master the skills you need to achieve your goals. If you don't embody something, you can't possibly know it. Ask yourself, "Am I a living example of...?" Stay open to learning new things and searching for things you may have overlooked. Last but not least, go back to basics when you don't get the results you want.

The Untapped Gold Mine

You're extremely valuable and have an unlimited potential for growth. The best investment you can make is in yourself. Not dedicating enough money and time to your personal growth indicates that you're devaluing yourself. Similarly, using your time unwisely shows a lack of self-respect. Your time is limited. It's not a free resource that those around you can use at will.

The Failure Myth

Successful people are willing to fail more than the average person. Failure can't be separated from success. It's an inherent part of the process of success. The only real failure is neglecting to learn from past "failures", or doing nothing due to fear of failure. If you continue to learn from your setbacks and improve over time, very few goals will be out of your reach.

Immersing Yourself in Your Goal

Be there years before it happens. No matter what your goal may be, visualize real-life situations that will be part of your reality when you achieve your goals. Learn to think, speak, and act as if you've already achieved them. What would you be doing? How would you feel? Who would be around you? Learn everything you can about your goal and surround yourself with people who have already achieved it, be it physically or virtually (YouTube videos etc.).

There are now just 6 days left. I encourage you to keep working hard on your goal during these 6 days. Perseverance is the most important thing right now. The focus will be on perseverance. Don't give up, even if you're far behind. Do your best. Even if you don't reach your goal see it as a way to develop greater grit and tenacity.

Day 85

Date: _____

Through perseverance many people win success out of what seemed destined to be certain failure.

— BENJAMIN DISRAELI

Daily goals

-
-
-
-
-
-

Daily tip: *Are you victim of the Parkinson law?*

The Parkinson "law" states that "works expand so has to fill the time available for its completion". If you have ever waited the last minute to write a paper for school, you know very well how this law works. The good news is that you still have a few more days to achieve your goals so why not start thinking of how you could use the remaining time as effectively as possible?

Question:

How can you move faster and increase your productivity?

Meetings/Appointments	People to contact
Chores	Things to purchase

Distraction crusher

Additional notes (insights, lessons learned etc.)

Day 86

Date: _____

> *Perseverance is the hard work you do after you get tired of doing the hard work you already did.*

— NEWT GINGRICH

Daily goals

-

-

-

-

-

-

Daily tip: *Grit is your friend.*

How much grit do you have? Grit has shown itself to be a key factor that, in many cases, can explain why some fail where others succeed. In her book *Grit*, author Angela Duckworth highlighted this fact in a study of Green Berets, 42% of whom gave up during the Special Force Selection Course. She found that grit was the best predictor of success. Some elements included in her Grit Scale are the ability to finish everything you start, focus on and complete a project that takes several months (or more!), and staying committed to the same goals for years.

Question:

How could you develop more grit in your life?

Meetings/Appointments	People to contact
Chores	Things to purchase

Distraction crusher

Additional notes (insights, lessons learned etc.)

Day 87

Date: _____

Great works are performed not by strength but by perseverance.

— SAMUEL JOHNSON

Daily goals

-

-

-

-

-

-

Daily tip: *Nana korobi ya oki.*

This Japanese proverb translates to "fall down seven times and get up eight." The Japanese are known for working hard and persevering. But persevering isn't just a Japanese thing. Anyone can develop perseverance over time, as is evidenced by the following Sylvester Stallone quote: *You, me, or nobody is gonna hit as hard as life. But it ain't about how hard ya hit. It's about how hard you can get hit and keep moving forward. How much you can take and keep moving forward. That's how winning is done!* When you fall down, make sure you always get up.

Empowering question:

What can you do to ensure that you'll always get up?

Meetings/Appointments	People to contact
Chores	Things to purchase

Distraction crusher

Additional notes (insights, lessons learned etc.)

Day 88

Date: _____

Patience and perseverance have a magical effect before which difficulties disappear and obstacles vanish.

— JOHN QUINCY ADAMS

Daily goals

-

-

-

-

-

-

Daily tip: *Be patient, be patient, be patient!*

"Be patient" would be a fantastic mantra to recite each day. Patience is so important when it comes to accomplishing anything worthwhile. Everything takes time, and, unfortunately, it often takes more time than we expect. Keep these two words in mind as you move towards your goal: **patience** and **perseverance.**

Empowering question:

What can you do each day to remind yourself to be patient?

Meetings/Appointments	People to contact
Chores	Things to purchase

Distraction crusher

Additional notes (insights, lessons learned etc.)

Day 89

Date: _____

Perseverance, secret of all triumphs.

— VICTOR HUGO

Daily goals

-

-

-

-

-

-

Daily tip: *Are you really trying?*

Most people say they tried, but did they really? In reality, the vast majority of people don't even get started. They pursue something for a few months before giving up. Or, maybe they try for a couple of years before giving up. Whatever the case is, giving up a few months into pursuing a goal that can take over a year isn't really trying. The same can be said for giving up a few years into pursuing a goal that can take over a decade to accomplish. If you genuinely want something, wouldn't it make sense to commit to working on it for more than a few months or years? Wouldn't you be willing to put in 5 years, a decade, or even more? Some people spend their entire lives working on what matters most to them, and sometimes that's what it takes. It's just a matter of how badly you want it.

Empowering question:

Can you commit to working on your most important goals regardless of how long they take to achieve?

Meetings/Appointments	People to contact
Chores	Things to purchase

Distraction crusher

Additional notes (insights, lessons learned etc.)

Day 90

Date: _____

It's not over until I win.

— LES BROWN

Daily goals

-

-

-

-

-

-

Daily tip: *It's not over until you win.*

This is a great mindset to have, and serves as another fantastic mantra. More often than not, our ability to persevere is what allows us to reach our goals when it seems like we're not going to make it. If your goal matters to you, learn to persevere more than anyone else. How? By understanding that you'll face far more challenges than you expect, and accepting the fact that this is perfectly normal. The key is to constantly learn, grow, and adapt. It's not over until it's over—it's not over until you win.

Empowering question:

Take the time to visualize potential challenges, then multiply them by 10. This will bring you closer to the truth of what you'll face.

Meetings/Appointments	People to contact
Chores	Things to purchase

Distraction crusher

Additional notes (insights, lessons learned etc.)

Monthly Goal Review ③ Final Review

You've made it to the end! Did you achieve your 90 goals? If you did, big congratulations! Make sure you celebrate with your family and friends.

If you didn't, still take some time to celebrate. You worked on your goal for 90 days and that's something that should be acknowledged! Sure, you may have missed some days, but you're still reading this. Remember that there's no such thing as 100 % consistency. We're only human. What matters is that you keep moving forward at your own pace. That's the process that counts.

Let's take some time to evaluate where you are regarding each topic we covered in this planner. Then we can see where you made progress and where you can improve. It's time to rate yourself on a scale of 1 to 10

1. Victim Mentality – How much responsibility do you take for your life?

Your score:

2. Social Conditioning – To what extent are you influenced by social conditioning?

Your score:

3. Harsh Realities – Have you accepted what it takes to be successful and the harsh reality of how difficult perseverance can be?

Your score:

4. Stickability – Are you committed to your goal? Are you confident that you'll keep working on it every day?

Your score:

5. Turning Your Goal into an Obsession – How often do you think of your goals?

Your score:

6. Welcoming Failure – Are you truly welcoming failure?

Your score:

7. Beating Procrastination – How often do you procrastinate?

Your score:

8. Adopting a Mastery Mindset – Do you dig deep and stay with your goal until you achieve it, or do you jump from one opportunity to another?

Your score:

9. Investing in Yourself – Do you value yourself? Are you willing to spend money in your own education?

Your score:

10. Taking Massive Action – Are you taking enough action? If you keep doing what you've done today, will you achieve your goal?

Your score:

11. Being There Before It Happens – Do you feel like you're already there? Do you have this strong sense of belief that you'll achieve your goal?

Your score:

12. Redesigning Your Environment – Is your environment making it easier for you to achieve your goal?

CONCLUSION

I'd like to thank you again for purchasing this goal-setting planner. More importantly, I'd like to congratulate you for sticking with me till the end! Setting daily goals for 90 days is no small achievement. You might not have been totally consistent with your goals, but don't worry too much. I'm still working on that, too. It's a never ending process.

By now, you should be equipped with everything you need to achieve your most exciting goals in the future. You've always had the inner resources necessary to make your dreams come true, my goal was to help you realize that.

I sincerely look forward to hearing from you and seeing the results you get in years to come. I'd be honored to have played a part in your future successes in some way. Don't hesitate to contact me at thibaut.meurisse@gmail.com in the future to share your story. Genuine testimonials will inspire people like you to use this planner to achieve their goals, too.

As for me, I'll keep working on my goals and doing my very best to help you and others.

I hope you'll follow me on my blog, watch my videos, and read some of my other books in the future. I'm on my own journey to actualize my potential and I hope that we'll keep growing together. If we stick to our goals, we'll be able to positively contribute to the world around us and leave it with no regrets.

My blog: *http://whatispersonaldevelopment.org*

My Facebook page:

https://www.facebook.com/whatispersonaldevelopment.org

My Amazon author page: *amazon.com/author/thibautmeurisse*

Let's keep in touch!

Thibaut Meurisse

Founder of whatispersonaldevelopment.org

BONUS SECTION

To further support you with your goals I included additional content at the end of this planner.

The bonus sections include the following:

- **My Daily Morning Ritual Checklist** – A section to help you create a powerful morning ritual
- **My Pledge to Become Unstoppable** – A section that will prevent you from giving up
- **My Limiting Beliefs Finder** – A section you can use to identify and eliminate disempowering beliefs
- **The Belief Shifter** – A section you can use to write down new, empowering beliefs
- **My "What If" Section** – A section to help you open up to new possibilities
- **The Most Powerful Affirmations** (organized by topic) – A section with the best affirmations on various topics, such as wealth, confidence, and persistence.
- **My Quarterly Goal Tracking Sheet** (add downloadable pdf)
- **A list of words to ban** from your vocabulary
- **A complete list of the daily tips** included in this planner
- **A blank section** to write down thoughts and ideas at any time
- **My Favorite Quotes Section** – A section where you're free to write down your favorite quotes

MY DAILY MORNING RITUAL

I started mine in June 2016 and have never looked back. Since you're already setting daily goals, you already have a morning ritual. It's just a matter of expanding it to better serve your goals and aspirations.

The benefits of daily morning rituals

A daily morning ritual can help you do the following:

- Take control of your life first thing in the morning by deciding each day how you want to feel and what you'd like to accomplish.
- Stack your most powerful habits together so that you don't skip them (goal setting, meditation, exercise, reading, etc.)
- Stay consistent on a daily basis to create exceptional, long-term results

3 Simple steps to create a daily morning ritual

You can create a daily morning ritual in 3 simple steps.

1. Decide how much time you want to dedicate to it. Is it 10 minutes? 30 minutes? 1 hour?

2. Decide exactly what you'll do. Start by selecting 2 or 3 things. Examples include:

- Setting daily goals (you're already doing that)
- Reading your long-term (as in monthly or yearly) goals
- Repeating affirmations
- Practicing gratitude
- Meditating
- Exercising

3. Perform your morning ritual first thing in the morning (before doing anything else).

One final tip: Commit to your morning ritual for a long period of time (ideally the rest of your life). If you're committed to creating a powerful morning ritual in your life, I encourage you to check my morning ritual book

Daily Morning Ritual Checklist

Write down the activities you'll do during your morning ritual

-

-

-
-
-
-

MY PLEDGE TO BECOME UNSTOPPABLE

MY PLEDGE TO BECOME UNSTOPPABLE

How often have you given up on your goals in the past? In this section, we're going to define the circumstances that could make you give up.

Take the time to answer the three questions below. They'll help you persevere with your goals.

Use a separate sheet of paper to brainstorm, then write your answer on this page when you're done.

What's the worst-case scenario I can think of? What would I do if it happened?

-

-

-

-

What precisely am I ready to go through before giving up on my goals? What would make me give up on them?

-

-

-

-

What will I do to ensure I don't quit when I feel like giving up?

-

-

-

-

MY LIMITING BELIEFS FINDER

What mental blocks are preventing you from reaching your potential in life?

Let me start by giving you a list of some common mental blocks and limiting beliefs that many people have. I took the liberty of briefly debunking them.

On self-esteem

- I'm not good enough → Did the doctor say that to your parents when you were born? I doubt it.
- I don't deserve to be successful → How often have you thought: I can do better than that guy? Or "Why is this person so successful? They're no better than me". Well, you're right. You deserve success as much as anyone else.

On money

- Money isn't important → Then why are you willing to spend 40+ years at a job you dislike or even hate? Would you still do that if you had more money?
- Money is the root of all evil → Absolutely not. Money is simply a means of expression. It acts as a magnifying glass revealing your true nature. Assholes become bigger assholes, good people do more good.
- Rich people are greedy → Some rich people are, but, on average, they're no greedier than "poor" people.
- There's something humble or respectable in being poor → Not particularly. Being poor doesn't require any effort, while creating your own wealth requires hard work. This belief sounds like something those in power would like the masses to believe. It's easier to control those who are poor and struggling than it is someone whose wealth and power are equal to yours.

Be your own person and realize that it's not wealth that makes someone good or bad, but rather the person's choices.

- I shouldn't make more money than my parents → Any parent in their right mind wants to see their child do better than they did. It's almost guaranteed that your parents will be proud of you. If they aren't, you can be proud of you, and that's all that matters.

On talent

- I have no talent → Any skill can be learned, and a mixture of hard work and persistence beats talent
- I'm not smart enough → You have an almost unlimited potential to grow. With enough work and repetition, you can master almost anything.

What limiting beliefs are

People act according to what they believe to be true. What you believe can put some serious limits on you. Your beliefs will be a determining factor in whether you'll achieve your goals. That's why you have to continually work on getting rid of disempowering beliefs and replacing them with new, empowered ones.

Identifying limiting beliefs

One of the simplest ways to overcome your limiting beliefs is to ask yourself the following questions:

- Why haven't I achieved my goals yet?
- What am I thinking when I experience negative emotions? (Your negative emotions are always the result of recurrent thoughts you have)

Overcoming your limiting beliefs

Here are 3 simple things you can do to overcome your limiting beliefs.

I. **Find examples that go against your limiting beliefs.** In your daily life, you will come across examples that shatter your beliefs. Be on the lookout for them.

2. Read books that will help you shift your beliefs. Read books related to what you're struggling with. If, for instance, you have a lot of disempowering beliefs about money, read books that will help you change them. You can start with *The Souls of Money* by Linn Twist and *Secrets of the Millionaire Mind* by T. Harv Eker.

3. Create positive affirmations and repeat them during your morning ritual. Create positive affirmations that will help you shift your current perspective. If you think money is bad, for instance, you could use the following affirmation:

Money is important because it allows me to... (give more to charity, spend more time with my family, invest in myself more, become a better person, etc.)

Additional tip: Keep a post-it on your desk or on the wall to remind you of your new beliefs and help you focus on them.

Write down your limiting beliefs

I encourage you to use this page to write down any disempowering beliefs that prevent you from getting the results you want in life. When you recognize a belief that isn't helping you, write it down.

THE BELIEF SHIFTER

In this section, write down any new empowering beliefs that you want to adopt.

Below are 3 examples of beliefs that I find particularly empowering.

1. If he can, I can

There's no fundamental difference between your brain and that of someone else's. If someone else has what you have, you can have it to. You'll need passion, perseverance, and a willingness to develop the skills you need to achieve your goals, but the fact remains that you can have what they have.

When I doubt my ability to make a career in my field (personal development), I always remind myself of how many people have successfully done it. They aren't smarter than me, they aren't more motivated than me, and they aren't working harder than me. My self-confidence and ability to persevere are what will ultimately determine my success, and that's true for you, too.

2. I'll succeed because so many people give up.

Achieving any goal involves some manner of competition. After all, there are thousands upon thousands of people that will strive to reach any given goal. Even so, the odds of you winning out aren't as bad as they sound.

Let's assume there are 100 people pursuing the same goal and only one of them can succeed. The first thing you have to realize is that many of them won't even get started. They won't buy the book, go the seminar, start working out, take lessons, or do anything related to the goal. They'll just procrastinate using the common "I'll to it someday". What about those who do start? Well, 90 to 95% of them will give up at some point. If, however, you continue setting goals every day and use the content of this book to build your skills, you won't be one of these people.

So, now that the majority have given up, there are only 5 to 10 people left. That's better! These 5 to 10 people will usually persevere long enough to enjoy some kind of results and even make some money out of it, provided it's a monetary goal like building the ideal career. The difference between these 5 to 10 people and the "winner" is the skills he or she will have developed during their personal development journey. These skills include believing in oneself, perseverance, goal obsession, self-discipline, and the constant desire to improve, to name just a few. As you can see, your chances are actually pretty good if you're sufficiently committed to your goal.

3. If 1, then 1 million

Let's assume you're working on your business and struggle for months to find your first client, but you get great feedback from them. The "If 1, then million" rule states that if one person likes something then millions of people around the world can like it, provided they're made aware of it. In other words, if you find your first client, then they are thousands or more waiting to buy your product or service, you just have to find them. Check out the examples below:

- If I can sell 1 copy of my book, then I can sell thousands or even millions of copies.
- If I can make $1 online, then I can make thousands or even millions of dollars online.
- If I can find 1 coaching clients, then I can find thousands or millions more.

This belief provides the following benefits:

- It gives you the motivation to persist until you find your first client, make your first dollar online, or whatever your first milestone is.
- It gives you the confidence to put yourself out there so you can sell more of your product or service, attract more clients, etc.
- It shows you that an increase in marketing is all you need to succeed. The product or service in itself is good enough.

For more on this subject, check out this video from my friend Joe by typing "You CAN live your Dream: Here's why you have a 66% chance!" in the Youtube search bar.

EMPOWERING BELIEF TO ADOPT

Ask yourself, "What must I believe to achieve my goal?" Write down your beliefs using the space below:

"WHAT IF" SECTION

This section allows you to ask yourself empowering questions to nurture your imagination and shift your beliefs. Remember that the more time you spend focusing on what you want, the better your results will be. As Tony Robbins says, "Quality questions create a quality life. Successful people ask better questions, and as a result, they get better answers."

Your mind will answer all your questions no matter how silly you may think they are. So, instead of asking questions like, "Why did this happen to me?" you could ask, "What can I learn from this?" or "What could I have done to avoid this situation?"

I suggest you use this section as a way to train yourself to come up with more empowering questions that will lift you up instead of dragging you down. You can be your best friend or your worst enemy. Make sure you go with the first option.

You can write some of your favorite questions down or you can ask yourself questions in your head. The choice is yours, but keep in mind that it will be more effective if you answer out loud and write down your answers.

Tip: I recommend starting your questions with the following words or phrases:

- What if...?
- What would I need to do to...?
- What could I do...?
- How...?
- Why + positive statements

Here are some examples:

- What if I could sell one million copies of my book?
- What if I could achieve my goal twice as fast?
- What if I could attract the perfect girl or guy in my life?
- What would I need to do to make a career out of my passion?
- What would I need to believe to achieve my goal?
- What could I do to add more value to people's lives?

- How can I become better?
- Why is my life so amazing?
- Why am I so blessed?

YOUR "WHAT IF" QUESTIONS

Use this page to write down your favorite empowering questions. Answer them on a regular basis.

POWERFUL AFFIRMATIONS

Here you'll find some great affirmations. Feel free to use those that resonate with you and create new ones.

On money/wealth

- I attract money in miraculous ways.
- The more people I help, the more wealth I create in my life.
- The more wealth I create, the more people I can help.
- Money allows incredible freedom in my life.
- I was wealthy yesterday, I am wealthy today, and I will be wealthy tomorrow.
- I can do a lot of good with my wealth; hence I stay wealthy.
- Whatever I do makes money for me.
- I'm always full of money.
- Being wealthy gives me joy, happiness, and peace of mind. I then give these things to those who need them.
- I am thankful for the abundance and prosperity in my life.

On confidence

- I love being confident.
- I am more and more confident each day.
- I am overflowing with joy, vitality, and energy — I'm unstoppable!
- I acknowledge my own self-worth; my confidence is soaring.

On success

- All that I need to be successful comes from within.
- I am solution-minded. Every problem is solvable.
- Success is my natural state of being. I think only of success.
- I utilize all ethical means to become successful. I leave no stone unturned.

- I am in charge of my emotions, desires, and abilities. I focus only on success.
- Success is an ongoing process. After one success, I focus on another.
- I am a man/woman of action and a man/woman of vision. As a result, everything I do ends in success.
- I let go of my need to chase success; I attract success by the person I become.

On gratitude

- I am continually amazed at how abundant my life already is!
- I am immensely grateful to be alive today.
- Every morning I give thanks and choose to be happy.
- I am truly thankful for my friends, family, and those who have been a positive part of my life.

On happiness

- I give myself permission to be happy, which gives me increased health, confidence, creativity, and attractiveness.
- I allow myself to be happy because it gives me the emotional strength to leave my comfort zone and achieve all my goals and dreams.
- Happiness is my natural state and I allow it to manifest in everything I do
- I touch many lives. My happiness makes others happy, thus making it one big, happy world.

On self-love

- Every day I give myself the gift of self-compassion and self-love.
- I love myself.
- I approve of and feel great about myself.

- My high self-esteem allows me to accept compliments easily while freely complimenting others.
- I accept others as they are and they accept me as I am.
- I release the need to prove myself to anyone because I am my own person. I wouldn't have it any other way!
- Unconditional love is the greatest gift I can give myself.
- I am proud of myself.

On goals

- I let go of a life without goals and replace it with a destiny of success and grand achievement.
- I accomplish everything I set out to do.
- I thoroughly enjoy the challenge of a meaningful, worthwhile goal.
- I enjoy the feeling of growth I experience each day as I work on my goals.
- I'm excited about my goals and the person they compel me to become.

On love/relationships

- I am here to learn to love myself and share that love with everyone around me.
- I am in a joyous, intimate relationship with someone who truly loves me.
- I am safe in all my relationships.
- I give and receive lots of love.
- My partner is the love of my life. We adore each other.
- I am very thankful for all the love in my life. I find it everywhere.

MY FAVORITE QUOTES

When you come across a quote that resonates with you, write it down here:

MY THOUGHT BANK

Use this section to write down any ideas, thoughts, or insights that you may have. This will increase your self-awareness and allow you to progress at a faster rate.

Words to ban from your vocabulary

The words you use when you talk to yourself and to others greatly influence your behavior. It works both ways. If you lack confidence, you'll say things like "I'll try", "Maybe", "I'm not sure", and so on. If you start using words that show confidence, such as "I will", "I'm going to do such and such", or "Definitely", you'll start acting accordingly. I started to work on this myself by changing the words I use in my emails. Each time I catch myself writing something like "Maybe" or "I'll try", I replace it with "I will" or "I'm going to".

Words and phrases to avoid

- Perhaps
- Maybe
- I'll try
- I hope
- I wish
- I'll give it a shot
- I think
- I believe
- I would like
- I might

Replace these words with "I will", "Definitely", "Certainly", "I'm going to", etc.

Replace phrases like "If", "One day", "Someday", and "If all goes well" with "When" statements. In other words, don't say "*If* I become a millionaire" say "*When* I become a millionaire."

Need vs. want

Replace "I need" with "I want". "I need" presupposes that something is lacking in your life, while "I want" simply expresses a desire for something. It's better to focus on what you want and why you want it instead of thinking that you "need" something.

"I *need* to get this done" becomes "I *want* to get this done" and "I *need* to achieve my goal" becomes "I *want* to achieve my goal"

Should vs. could

There's nothing that you "should" do in your life. Thinking that you "should" do something generally means that you're trying to do what others want you to do rather than what you want to do. Is telling yourself that you "should" do something inspiring you? Probably not. With that in mind, something like "I should work harder" needs to become "I *could* work harder" (if it's a possibility you're considering) or "I *want* to work harder" (if you've decided it's something that *you* want).

OTHER BOOKS BY THE AUTHORS:

Crush Your Limits: Break Free from Limitations and Achieve Your True Potential

Goal Setting: The Ultimate Guide to Achieving Life-Changing Goals (Free Workbook Included)

Habits That Stick: The Ultimate Guide to Building Habits That Stick Once and For All (Free Workbook Included)

Master Your Emotions: A Practical Guide to Overcome Negativity and Better Manage Your Feelings (Free Workbook Included)

Productivity Beast: An Unconventional Guide to Getting Things Done (Free Workbook Included)

The Greatness Manifesto: Overcome Your Fear and Go After What You Really Want

The One Goal: Master the Art of Goal Setting, Win Your Inner Battles, and Achieve Exceptional Results (Free Workbook Included)

The Passion Manifesto: Escape the Rat Race, Uncover Your Passion and Design a Career and Life You Love

The Thriving Introvert: Embrace the Gift of Introversion and Live the Life You Were Meant to Live (Free Workbook Included)

Upgrade Yourself: Simple Strategies to Transform Your Mindset, Improve Your Habits and Change Your Life

Wake Up Call: How To Take Control Of Your Morning And Transform Your Life (Free Workbook Included)

ABOUT THE AUTHOR

THIBAUT MEURISSE

Thibaut Meurisse is a personal development blogger, author, and founder of whatispersonaldevelopment.org.

He has been featured on major personal development websites such as Lifehack, Goalcast, TinyBuddha, Addicted2Success, MotivationGrid or PickTheBrain.

Obsessed with self-improvement and fascinated by the power of the brain, his personal mission is to help people realize their full potential and reach higher levels of fulfillment and consciousness.

In love with foreign languages, he is French, writes in English, and lived in Japan for almost ten years.

Learn more about Thibaut at:

amazon.com/author/thibautmeurisse
whatispersonaldevelopment.org
thibaut.meurisse@gmail.com

Made in the USA
Las Vegas, NV
05 March 2021

19081969R00233